Evidence-Based Approaches to Peace and Conflict Studies

Volume 14

This series aims to publish books on peace and conflict with evidence-based approaches, befitting an era best characterized by uncertainty and complexity. Even if occurrence of major wars among sovereign states has dramatically decreased, from 5 million soldiers killed between 1938 and 1945 per annum; through 100,000 soldiers killed between 1945 and 1989 per annum; to 10,000 soldiers killed between 1989 and 2019 per annum; many kinds of peace and conflict keep arising in the world, with extraordinary technological progress and unprecedented spatial coverage. All parts of the world now are so well connected and interdependent. At the same time, they easily and suddenly become sources of immense vulnerability and fragility, bringing one or another of them to the verge of collapse and destruction. The causes are diverse: climate change, migration, pandemic and epidemic disease, civil strife, religious dissonance, economic competition, arms races, terrorism, corruption—a virtual plethora of sources. Kofi Annan, former UN Secretary General, calls these and many others "problems without passports."

The basic methodological orientation sought in this series is broadly that of modern social and behavioral science. Of importance is that verifiable evidence (quantitative and qualitative, graphs and photos) be solidly attached to whatever arguments are advanced.

Overseen by a panel of renowned scholars led by Editor-in-Chief Takashi Inoguchi, this book series employs a single-blind review process in which the Editor-in-Chief, the series editors, editorial board members, and specialized scholars designated by the Editor-in-Chief or series editors rigorously review each proposal and manuscript to ensure that every submission makes a valuable contribution that will appeal to a global scholarly readership.

Motomichi Igarashi

War and Data on Armed Conflicts

Global Networks Examining Casualties

Springer

Motomichi Igarashi
Faculty of Policy Studies
Kansai University
Suita, Osaka, Japan

ISSN 2730-5651 ISSN 2730-566X (electronic)
Evidence-Based Approaches to Peace and Conflict Studies
ISBN 978-981-97-6417-4 ISBN 978-981-97-6418-1 (eBook)
https://doi.org/10.1007/978-981-97-6418-1

The translation was done with the help of an artificial intelligence machine translation tool. A subsequent human revision was done primarily in terms of content.

Translation from the Japanese language edition: "Sensō to dēta—Shisha wa ikani sūchi to nattaka" by Motomichi Igarashi, © Motomichi Igarashi, 2023. Published by CHUOKORON-SHINSHA.INC. All Rights Reserved.

This Springer imprint is published by the registered company Springer Nature Singapore Pte Ltd.
The registered company address is: 152 Beach Road, #21-01/04 Gateway East, Singapore 189721, Singapore

Preface

Many phenomena in international politics cannot be directly observed. For example, while wars occur in certain regions, it is impossible for a single individual to experience the entire phenomenon of war. Indeed, numerous soldiers engage in armed combat, while civilians often find themselves displaced as refugees amid the conflict. But while both of their experiences are extremely important for understanding war, they only represent a small part of war and cannot explain its entirety. Not limited to war, the scale of phenomena in international politics is simply too large. A macroscopic explanation that goes beyond individual experiences is thus inevitably necessary.

We have sought to understand the whole picture by converting various international political phenomena, including wars, into data. For instance, there is a wide variety of data related to international politics, such as the number of war casualties, refugees, infant mortality rates, maternal mortality rates, and the population living below the poverty line.

The demand for such data collection has been increasing since the 2000s. A prime example is the Sustainable Development Goals (SDGs), which include numerous goals for the international community to work towards by 2030, encompassing 232 different indicators to numerically grasp progress. As represented by the SDGs, if one were to summarize the 2020s, when this book was written, in a single phrase, it could be called the "age of facts." This is because many people believe that all policies should be formulated and evaluated based on facts, or concrete data.

However, while policies require facts, fake news has become a grave problem worldwide. In 2016, Oxford University Press selected "post-truth" as the word of the year. The internet is flooded with unverified information, prompting people to launch various election campaigns and social movements. Society is also showing a vector opposite to the emphasis on facts. It is said that individual literacy is necessary to deal with unverified information, but how can we enhance literacy about data in international politics?

This book considers data on armed conflicts (DAC) among the diverse data on international politics. War is one of the worst phenomena in international politics; therefore, data collection is inevitably necessary to grasp the whole picture of war.

However, to what extent does war data reflect the actual phenomenon? In other words, while someone somewhere in the world is suffering from war, how accurately does that data represent the war that they are experiencing? Who is creating that DAC, for what purpose, and how? If there are events in war that are converted into data and those that are not, how are they selected? Can we truly understand the reality of war from data? These are the questions this book poses and aims to answer. Considering that DAC itself is a part of information warfare and that fake news is rampant today, these questions are extremely important. This book focuses on the link between war and DAC.

However, there are not many studies that analyze the entire structure of DAC generation. One valuable preceding study is *Violence, Statistics, and the Politics of Accounting for the Dead*, edited by Pérouse de Montclos (Cham: Springer, 2016), which discusses the methodology of casualty investigation in a cross-disciplinary manner. However, the overall structure of war data generation remains unclear. Research on DAC is scattered across various fields and disciplines, such as conflict studies, international law, statistics, and forensic science, making it difficult to grasp the overall picture. Therefore, this book presents a meaningful schematic for understanding DAC. Specifically, it sheds light on the international norms that DAC relies on, the actors who generate the data, and the various scientific methods that these actors use. To do this, it refers to studies on war and international law, as well as statistics, forensic science, and research on chemical weapons. In addition, this book adopts a historical approach to analyzing the structure of war data generation. A similar study is Helen M. Kinsella's *The Image before the Weapon: A Critical History of the Distinction between Combatant and Civilian* (Ithaca: Cornell University Press, 2011). However, Kinsella's study is an analysis of the concept of civilian protection, not a study of DAC.

The analytical perspective of this book is similar to the research field of Science and Technology Studies (STS), which analyzes the relationship between society and scientific knowledge and technology. Science was once considered value-neutral, and superior scientific knowledge was thought to lead to optimal practices and policies. However, since the 1970s, researchers in STS have begun to challenge this view by analyzing in detail who generates specific scientific knowledge and technology, how they are generated, and how they relate to society; according to these researchers, in the world of science, hypotheses and theories often remain unresolved, making scientific knowledge and technology uncertain. They have also revealed that such hypotheses and theories have been significantly influenced by politics, society, and economics. In the 2000s, researchers in this field have been striving to reestablish the social significance of expert knowledge.

DAC is sometimes a serious matter involving the use of military force. For example, if a major power hopes to militarily intervene in a conflict in a certain region on the grounds that chemical weapons have been used, the war data stating "chemical weapons have been used" can become the trigger. However, despite its importance, it has not been sufficiently analyzed who has generated DAC and how. This book, like STS, points out that much of war data is uncertain while also highlighting the struggles of those who have tried to apply scientific durability to DAC. It thus intends to clarify that there is sufficient social significance of expert knowledge in this field.

Osaka, Japan Motomichi Igarashi
July 2024

Contents

About the Author

Dr. Motomichi Igarashi received his Ph.D. in International Relations from the University of Sussex in 2013. Since then, he has conducted research and lectured on security issues at Hokkaido University and Kansai University. In 2023, he was appointed Professor of International Relations at the School of Policy Studies, Kansai University.

In 2016, he published his first solo-authored book, *Humanitarianism and Trusteeship: From Colonial Administration to Peace Building*, in Japanese. This book, based on his doctoral dissertation submitted to the University of Sussex, garnered attention for its innovative analysis of power structures in peacebuilding and was reviewed in various newspapers and journals. In 2023, he published his second solo-authored book, *War and Data: How the Dead Became Numbers*, in Japanese, which earned him the Osaragi Jiro Rondan Award for 2023. The Osaragi Jiro Rondan Award is an academic prize sponsored by the major Japanese newspaper Asahi Shimbun, awarded to the most outstanding book in the fields of politics and economics within a year.

Dr. Igarashi has authored various papers on security issues, including "Scientific Data on Civilian Casualties and International Criminal Court" (2020), "U.S. Reluctant Interventions and Sovereignty" (2019), and "The Struggle over the Representation of Armed Conflicts: Human Rights NGOs, Sovereign States, and Post-Colonial Conflicts" (2018). All of these papers are peer-reviewed and written in Japanese.

Regarding research funding, he has received grants four times from the Ministry of Education, Culture, Sports, Science and Technology, and once from a private organization. His current research project analyzes the impact of digital witnesses on the generation of armed conflict data, supported by a grant from the Ministry of Education, Culture, Sports, Science and Technology (2022–2025).

Abbreviations

AAAS	American Association for the Advancement of Science
CEH	Comisión para el Esclarecimiento Histórico
CHR	UN Commission on Human Rights
CIIDH	Centro Internacional para Investigaciones en Derechos Humanos
CSCE	Conference on Security and Cooperation in Europe
DAC	Data on Armed Conflicts
FDR	Frente Democrático Revolucionario
FMLN	Frente Farabundo Martí para la Liberación Nacional
FSA	Free Syrian Army
GBD	Global Burden of Disease
HRMMU	UN Human Rights Monitoring Mission in Ukraine
ICC	International Criminal Court
ICMP	International Commission on Missing Persons
ICRC	International Committee of the Red Cross
ICTR	International Criminal Tribunal for Rwanda
ICTY	International Criminal Tribunal for the former Yugoslavia
IFOR	Implementation Force
IHME	Institute for Health Metrics and Evaluation
MSE	Multiple Systems Estimation
OHCHR	Office of the High Commissioner for Human Rights
OPCW	Organization for the Prohibition of Chemical Weapons
PHR	Physicians for Human Rights
REMHI	Recuperación de la Memoria Histórica
SNC	Syrian National Council
UNDP	United Nations Development Programme
UNMOVIC	United Nations Monitoring, Verification and Inspection Commission
UNPROFOR	United Nations Protection Force
UNSCOM	United Nations Special Commission

UNSMIS	United Nations Supervision Mission in Syria
UNYOM	UN Yemen Observation Mission
WHO	World Health Organization

Chapter 1
Introduction: Doubting Expert Opinions

Contents

Abstract This chapter highlights the often uncertain and inconclusive nature of international political data. It specifically examines the number of deaths caused by malaria and the proportion of civilian deaths in armed conflicts. In response to such uncertainty, this book adopts a position of critical functionalism. This perspective analyzes data from three aspects: scientific durability, social reliability, and functionality, and questions their degrees. The book states that data in international politics cannot be judged by a binary of true or false. Furthermore, this chapter introduces a model where the reality of war is converted into data on armed conflict (DAC) through international norms and the scientific analytical process. In addition, it introduces the concept of a humanitarian network as a collective of actors deeply involved in the development of international norms and the scientific analytical process.

One day, a certain university professor was preparing for a class. He was researching the war in Bosnian-Herzegovina that occurred in the 1990s, but was struggling to identify the minimum amount of information he should convey to his students about this war. First, he needed to clarify where the war took place, how long it lasted, and who the involved actors were. He also thought he needed to research the number of war casualties, but when he searched on the internet he found a figure of 200,000, while further research also revealed a figure of 100,000. The professor was at a loss. After all, how many people lost their lives in this war? Why do such differences arise?

This professor is a model of the author, but there may be quite a few people who have had such experiences. Data on international politics is diverse, but even experts find it difficult to select the most reliable data. Before entering the discussion of this book, it is pertinent to examine the concept of "fluctuation" in data within the realm of international politics. It is essential to identify the types of data that

M. Igarashi, *War and Data on Armed Conflicts*, Evidence-Based Approaches to Peace and Conflict Studies 14, https://doi.org/10.1007/978-981-97-6418-1_1

exhibit fluctuations and to analyze the mechanisms through which these fluctuations manifest.

1.1 Uncertainty of International Political Data

Different Numbers of Malaria Deaths

Data on international politics is diverse, but the connected field of health and hygiene is particularly active in discussions about data. Health and hygiene data, for example, include known infant mortality rates, maternal mortality rates, and prevalence rates of specific infectious diseases in each country. Data is essential for evaluating the progress and results of health and hygiene policies by nations and international organizations, and policy budgets can change significantly depending on the data. Therefore, data often becomes a field where the interests of related actors collide. First, by examining health and hygiene data, I aim to explore the inherent uncertainty present in such data.

In 2012, the Institute for Health Metrics and Evaluation (IHME) at the University of Washington announced the results of the Global Burden of Disease Study (GBD). Included in the survey results was data on the number of deaths from malaria, which caused controversy in the world of health and sanitation. According to the survey results, the number of deaths worldwide from malaria was about 995,000 in 1980, then rose to 1,817,000 in 2004, and decreased to 1,238,000 in 2010.[1] What does this change in numbers mean?

Malaria is a disease that is transmitted by being bitten by a mosquito carrying the malaria parasite. This disease has plagued humanity for many years. The World Health Organization (WHO) embarked on a malaria eradication program for over ten years from 1955, but despite investing massive funds and personnel, it failed to achieve its goal.[2] Then, in the late 1990s, the WHO, in collaboration with the World Bank, UNICEF, UNDP, and others, launched malaria control measures in middle and low-income countries.[3] The WHO has been regularly collecting and publishing related data on malaria, including the number of deaths, but this is significantly different from the aforementioned survey results by IHME in 2012.

Both the WHO data and the IHME data agree that 2004 was the peak year for deaths from malaria, however, the numbers from both organizations were significantly different. For example, for the number of deaths from malaria in 2010, IHME reported 1,238,000, while the WHO's 2011 report stated 655,000, almost twice the

---

[1] Christopher J. L. Murray, Lisa C. Rosenfeld, Stephen S. Lim, Kathryn G. Andrews, Kyle J. Foreman, Diana Haring, Nancy Fullman, Mohsen Naghavi, Rafael Lozano, and Alan D. Lopez, "Global Malaria Mortality between 1980 and 2010: A Systematic Analysis," *Lancet* 379 (2012): 413.

[2] Taira Nishi, *Global Health Law: Principles and History* (Nagoya: Nagoya University Press, 2022) [Japanese], 164–73.

[3] Ibid., 273.

difference. Furthermore, while the WHO stated that 86% of malaria deaths were in children under five years of age,[4] IHME estimated it to be around 57%.[5] In other words, the WHO data suggested that malaria is a problem for infants, while the IHME data suggested that it is a serious cause of death not limited to this age range.

Political Influence and Differences in Data Generation Methods

The year 2012 was a groundbreaking year for health and hygiene data. This was the year when IHME first announced its survey results to the world, which greatly changed the world of health and hygiene. IHME was established in 2007 by Christopher Murray, a health and hygiene data expert, with financial assistance from the Bill & Melinda Gates Foundation, at the University of Washington. Murray was originally a researcher at Harvard University who worked for WHO from 1998 to 2003, involved in a project to compare and rank the functional status of healthcare systems in various countries. This was supposed to enable a comparison of healthcare system levels worldwide, but it sparked political controversy and since then the WHO has stopped publishing such rankings. Deeply hurt by this outcome, Murray returned to Harvard University from WHO in 2003 and decided to establish an academic research institution that would generate health and hygiene data without political interference. The resulting organization that was created with the support of Bill Gates is IHME.[6]

The difference between IHME and WHO data was not just in the number of malaria deaths, with differences also seen in maternal mortality rates. What did the differences in survey results between IHME and WHO mean? There has been some criticism that WHO's health and hygiene data is susceptible to political influence and is uncertain because it has not undergone sufficient scientific peer review,[7] while IHME was considered less susceptible to pressure from the countries it analyzed compared to WHO. Thus, the survey results by IHME in 2012 sparked a major controversy.[8]

While we will not make enquiries deeper into the issue of health and hygiene data here, this case is rich in implications about data. Firstly, the generation of data related to international politics can be influenced by politics. Data from international organizations, not limited to the WHO, cannot always be said to be "unaffected by political influence, always neutral." For example, in 2021, it was reported that there

---

[4] World Health Organization, *World Malaria Report 2011* (Geneva: Word Health Organization, 2011), 73.

[5] Murray et al., *Global Malaria Mortality*, 425.

[6] With the establishment of IHME, Murray transferred to the University of Washington. Jeremy N. Smith, *Epic Measures: One Doctor. Seven Billion Patients* (New York: Harper Collins Publishers, 2015).

[7] Manjari Mahajan, "The IHME in the Shifting Landscape of Global Health Metrics," *Global Policy* 10, Supplement 1 (2019): 112.

[8] For the difference in data between IHME and WHO, refer to Mahajan, "The IHME in the Shifting Landscape," and also Marlee Tichenor and Devi Sridhar, "Metric Partnerships: Global Burden of Disease Estimates within the World Bank, the World Health Organisation and the Institute for Health Metrics and Evaluation," *Wellcome Open Research* 4, no. 35 (2020).

was manipulation in the "Doing Business Ranking" published annually by the World Bank, such as the unjustified elevation of the rankings of China and Saudi Arabia.[9] Just because it is data from an international organization does not mean it is fair, neutral, and trustworthy. The generation of data is never unrelated to politics.

Secondly, even if there is no political influence, differences in data generation methods can potentially lead to significant differences in results. The problem is that this is difficult to understand for anyone other than experts. IHME used a more complex statistical process for data generation than WHO, and it was thus difficult for non-experts to understand what this specifically entailed, resulting in criticisms that it was opaque.[10] So far, IHME has announced its survey results in *The Lancet*, a globally authoritative peer-reviewed medical journal, with peer reviews naturally conducted before publication; its data, which is scientifically durable, should have been published. However, because the number of researchers involved in IHME's survey is so large, it has become very difficult to find independent experts.

What Percentage Are Civilian Casualties?

What I have just mentioned was about health and hygiene data, but what about war data, the theme of this book? Perhaps the most contentious issue has been the "percentage of civilian casualties in war." Here, civilians are defined as individuals who do not belong to organizations such as the military and do not have the ability to retaliate even if they are caught up in combat.

As detailed in Chap. 3, international humanitarian law stipulates that civilians should not be intentionally targeted in war. Yet in actual wars, there are countless cases of civilians dying as a result of being caught up in combat, and thus the number of civilians are dying in wars has been a topic of discussion among researchers and practitioners. The particular issue was the thesis put forward by some researchers and practitioners that "in wars since the end of the Cold War, civilian casualties account for eighty (or ninety) percent of all casualties." Is this thesis true or false? Are the numbers real? What is it based on? This point has been previously addressed by international political scientists such as Adam Roberts, however, in this context, I intend to revisit what I deem to be relevant materials, drawing upon their discussions for further analysis.[11]

One of the origins of the debate was Mary Kaldor, who presented her theory of "new wars" in 1999. She pointed out that in wars after the end of the Cold War, 80% of the casualties were civilians. Her new wars theory argues that after the end of the Cold War, new types of civil wars influenced by globalization have become the mainstream form of warfare. In these new wars, political struggles over identities

[9] Yuka Hayashi, "World Bank Says Managers Pressured Staff to Alter Global Business Rankings," *The Wall Street Journal*, December 17, 2020.

[10] Mahajan, "The IHME in the Shifting Landscape," 115–17.

[11] Adam Roberts, "Lives and Statistics: Are 90% of War Victims Civilians?" *Survival* 52, no. 3 (June–July 2010), 115–36; Kelly M. Greenhill, "Counting the Cost: The Politics of Numbers in Armed Conflict," in Peter Andreas and Kelly M. Greenhill, *Sex, Drugs, and Body Counts: The Politics of Numbers in Global Crime and Conflict* (Ithaca and London: Cornell University Press, 2010).

such as ethnicity and religion have become the main points of conflict, and many civilians have thus become targets of attack. This discussion of new wars had a significant impact on security studies and policy.

In her book *New and Old Wars*, Kaldor states the following:

> At the beginning of the twentieth century, 85-90 per cent of casualties in war were military. In World War II, approximately half of all war deaths were civilian. By the late 1990s, the proportions of a hundred years ago have been almost exactly reversed, so that nowadays approximately 80 per cent of all casualties in wars are civilian.[12]

In new wars, because political struggles over identity are the main points of conflict, the distinction between soldiers/civilians is less important than differences in ethnicity or religion. Therefore, ordinary citizens become targets of attack.

The problem is the description that "80% of the casualties are ordinary citizens." Kaldor notes that she calculated the 80% figure herself,[13] so what data was the basis for this calculation? Kaldor explains this in the introduction to *Restructuring the Global Military Sector, Volume I: New Wars* (1997)[14]; according to her, the data sources are *World Military and Social Expenditures, 16th edition* (1996), by economist Ruth Leger Sivard, and *The State of War and Peace Atlas* (1997), by Dan Smith of the Oslo International Peace Research Institute.[15]

What is written in Sivard's *World Military and Social Expenditures, 16th edition*? In the section on war in the book, Sivard writes that "Today [from 1900 to 1995], more than 90% of all casualties are non-combatants."[16] Confusingly, while Kaldor states 80%, Sivard states 90%. There is a table of wars and war-related deaths that occurred between 1900 and 1995 (i.e., the entire twentieth century), with the number of civilian deaths in each war listed (if no data is available, it is not listed).[17] Presumably, Kaldor calculated based on this table.

What is the data source for this table? The note explains that it is an update of the records provided by William Eckhardt for the eighth edition of the same book in 1982.[18] However, the eighth edition mainly discusses the 1970s, and the armed conflicts of the 1990s had not yet occurred. Also, Eckhardt died in 1992, so any data after that was not updated by him. Looking back at the editions, the fourteenth edition

---

[12] Mary Kaldor, *New and Old Wars: Organized Violence in a Global Era* (Cambridge: Polity Press, 1999), 100.

[13] Ibid., 165.

[14] Mary Kaldor, "Introduction," in *Restructuring Theveen Global Military Sector, Volume I: New Wars*, ed. Mary Kaldor and Basker Vashee, 9. London and Washington: Pinter, 1997.

[15] In addition to the 1997 report, there is also a description in Edmund Cairns, *A Safer Future: Reducing the Human Costs of War* (Oxford: Oxfam Insight series, 1997), 17, that civilians account for 84% of casualties in modern warfare. Also, in the European Platform for Conflict Prevention and Transformation, *Prevention and Management of Violent Conflicts, 1998 Edition* (Utrecht: European Platform for Conflict Prevention and Transformation, 1998), 17, it is stated that civilians account for more than 90% of casualties in post-Cold War conflicts.

[16] Ruth Leger Sivard, *World Military and Social Expenditures, 16th edition* (Washington DC: World Priorities, 1996), 17.

[17] Ibid., 18–19.

[18] Ibid., 54.

(1991) states "in 1990 [the proportion of civilian deaths] appears to have been close to 90%."[19] This edition was just before Eckhardt's death, and again, the note explains that it is based on the numbers he recorded,[20] with mention elsewhere that references could not be included due to margin constraints. From this, it can be understood that various documents collected by Eckhardt at least serve as the data source. Sivard (or Eckhardt) noted that such civilian death numbers were not necessarily reliable data, and their values were merely for reference.

What about *The State of War and Peace Atlas* (1997) by Dan Smith of the Oslo International Peace Research Institute? It states the following about war deaths, along with a world map: "There were about five and a half million war deaths in the first half of the 1990s. Three quarters of them were civilians, including a million children."[21] In other words, this book estimates that 75% of the war deaths were civilians, which is slightly different from Kaldor. And again, there are notes that the number of war deaths is not very reliable, with hardly any agencies counting civilian deaths in most wars. So, what is the data source for these numbers? According to the book, the numbers were calculated by combining news media including international news agencies and official documents.[22]

So, how accurate are the numbers presented by Sivard and Smith? To consider this, we should examine the mortality data resulting from the conflict in Bosnia-Herzegovina that occurred in the early 1990s. Sivard states that the number of deaths in this conflict was 263,000,[23] in contrast to Smith who says that "200,000 was the safe figure, the common currency."[24] Smith says that in the late 1990s, many people used the number 200,000, while some argued for even larger numbers, however, subsequent research suggested that a more realistic figure was "100,000" (the basis for this number will be discussed in Chap. 5). Thus, it is not easy to determine how accurately the numbers circulating among researchers reflect reality.

The statement that "80% (or 90%) of the victims were civilians" can be found in sources other than Kaldor's argument and the literature she referred to. One of the first documents to present this figure is a 1991 report by the Stockholm International Peace Research Institute, which contains the following passage: "In a recent report it was estimated that, in the major conflicts waged in 1988–89, 9 of 10 victims since the start of the conflicts were civilian."[25] There are two points to note here. First, the analysis is based on wars before 1990, which is different from the argument introduced earlier. Second, the "victims" include not only the dead but also displaced people such as refugees. It is not clear from this report what percentage are dead.

---

[19] Ruth Leger Sivard, *World Military and Social Expenditures, 14 edition* (Washington DC: World Priorities, 1991), 20.

[20] Ibid., 60.

[21] Dan Smith, *The State of War and Peace Atlas* (London: Penguin, 1997), 24–25.

[22] Ibid., 100.

[23] Sivard, *World Military and Social Expenditures, 16th edition*, 18.

[24] Smith, *The State of War and Peace Atlas*, 100.

[25] Stockholm International Peace Research Institute (SIPRI), *Yearbook 1991: World Armaments and Disarmament* (New York: Oxford University Press, 1991), 349.

What is the source of the data? It is based on the results of a survey conducted by Uppsala University in Sweden in cooperation with the Red Cross, titled *Casualties of Conflict* (1991). The book analyzes civilian casualties as follows:

> Three out of four deaths are civilian in the conflict locations where distribution of civilian and military deaths is listed (i.e. 13 locations, covering about 50% of all deaths).
>
> For the other 23 locations with no available figures, a "conservative" assumption (lower than in the 13 locations) of an equal distribution between civilian and military deaths can be made.
>
> This gives the result that nine out of ten of all victims (dead and uprooted) are civilian."[26]

This report refers to the 1989 and 1990 reports of the Stockholm International Peace Research Institute and the U.S. Committee for Refugees' *World Refugee Survey–1989 in Review* to derive this figure.[27] However, it is unclear which parts of these reports were referred to and how.

UNICEF was another organization that discussed civilian casualties based on this report from Uppsala University. The organization's *The State of the World's Children 1996* states: "In the last decades of this century the proportion of civilian victims has been rising steadily: in World War II it was two thirds, and by the end of the 1980s it was almost 90 per cent."[28] However, it is not clear what is included in this category of "victims" from this report alone.

Such figures as "90% of the victims are civilians" were also found in reports from Uppsala University and the Stockholm International Peace Research Institute. However, unlike the discussions of Kaldor and others, these were analyzing wars before 1990. Also, it was not just a percentage of the number of deaths, but a percentage that included people who were displaced from their homes.

After all, what percentage of civilian casualties were there in the wars of the 1990s? How much do figures like 80% or 90% reflect reality? Just by tracing the data sources of the literature, it is not immediately possible to judge their accuracy. As will be discussed in the following chapters, there is not necessarily a lot of scientifically reliable data on armed conflicts (DAC), with several reasons for this. First, it is difficult to generate DAC. The battlefield is always dangerous, so people collecting data cannot operate freely; even the fighting armies themselves sometimes cannot do that. Needless to say, it is dangerous for a neutral third party to enter from outside and investigate. Secondly, DAC is closely related to national security, so the parties involved do not necessarily disclose accurate data. In the Ukraine War that broke out in 2022, Russia has hardly disclosed the number of its own military deaths. This is common historically, and in some cases, false information is deliberately disclosed, meaning DAC cannot be easily believed. However, if there is no other data, you have to use it, which is how distortions in the data occur.

---

[26] C. Ahlstrom and K. A. Nordquist, *Casualties of Conflict* (Uppsala: Department of Peace and Conflict Research, Uppsala University, 1991), 18–19.

[27] Ibid., 18.

[28] UNICEF, *The State of the World's Children 1996* (Oxford: Oxford University Press, 1996), 13.

Three Positions on Data on Armed Conflicts

How should we deal with the uncertainty of DAC? Here, I present three positions that can be logically considered.

Nihilism

This is the first position to consider is that all DAC does not sufficiently reflect reality, which this book calls "nihilism." This position believes that there is political influence on all data: the influence of the self-interest of the person who generated the data, as well as interference from others related to the data. Although it is not DAC, the data manipulation in the World Bank's "Doing Business Ranking" is an example, while there may also be the influence of bias that unconsciously occurs when generating data. Nihilism is correct in a sense. All data may be subject to political and bias influences. Identifying these issues may lead to the generation of more accurate data.

However, over-skepticism of data can also cause problems. For example, suppose the United Nations announces that chemical weapons were used in the Syrian conflict and, in response, Russia claims that this was a false report. Which claim is correct? According to nihilism, one might think, "Both the UN's claim and Russia's claim are suspicious. The truth is in the dark," but is that really okay? Or, if a human rights NGO announces the total number of civilian deaths in the Iraq War but then ignores that number for the reason that it is scientifically uncertain, what then? Ignoring data because it is uncertain could lead to further problematic scenarios.

Optimism

In contrast to nihilism, one could consider the position of believing all DAC, which this book calls "optimism." According to optimism, there is no point in doubting DAC every time, so one should assume that it is correct and act accordingly. Indeed, there is some truth to this position. When thinking about war, if everyone doubts and verifies all data every time, there is no end. If one assumes that states, the UN, and NGOs are all reporting falsely for their own interests, no policy can be evaluated. And giving up on collecting DAC could lead to giving up on thinking about war itself. Therefore, the position of optimism, which accepts data as correct for the sake of saving the trouble of verification, emerges.

However, this position also has problems. In the case of DAC, there are often multiple conflicting data, with the number of civilian casualties a prime example. For instance, in the Afghanistan War that broke out in 2001, consider if the U.S. military caused massive civilian casualties due to a bombing error. In this case, if the data from the U.S. military, NGOs, and the UN are all different, it is not possible to believe all of them because contradictions arise. However, it also cannot be said that averaging them will get closer to the truth and, therefore, it is not always possible to accept all data with optimism.

Critical Functionalism

This book presents a third position against these "nihilism" and "optimism," "critical functionalism,"[29] which aims to relativize the dichotomy of "correct data/wrong data" as much as possible. DAC cannot be simply divided into correct or incorrect; while it is nearly impossible to collect completely accurate data on the battlefield, that does not mean that the generation of data itself is impossible. It is undesirable for issues to be ignored due to a lack of data and, therefore, while paying attention to accuracy, it is necessary to accept some data. For this purpose, critical functionalism examines data from three analytical perspectives.

First, the scientific durability of the data. As this book will reveal, DAC is diverse. There is data that counts the number of war deaths, data that reveals how the deceased died, the cause, and legal responsibility, and data that investigates the type and condition of the weapons used (for example, chemical weapons) to determine whether there has been a violation of international law, each of which has its own scientific knowledge and experts. When looking at DAC, it is necessary to examine who generated the data, by what scientific method, through what process, and to judge the level of scientific durability of the data. Scientific durability cannot be judged as "present/absent"; ultimately, it is judged on the basis of comparing multiple data and determining whether it is relatively high or low.

Second, the social credibility of the data. The awkward part of human nature is that just because the data is scientifically correct, it does not mean that it is easily believed. When an infectious disease spreads, even if the information is scientifically durable, it can be drowned out by rumors. Similarly, even if DAC is scientifically durable, it does not necessarily mean that society will accept it. When looking at DAC, understanding the nature of the data by judging whether its social credibility is relatively low or high is crucial. As mentioned in Chap. 5, regarding the war in Bosnian-Herzegovina, as a result of research, the figure of 100,000 war deaths was considered to have the highest scientific durability, but it was not immediately accepted socially. Society needs some narrative when it experiences war: why the war occurred, who fought in what way, and who died. This narrative often becomes a battleground for the legitimacy of the survivors. Therefore, scientific durability does not necessarily correlate with social credibility.

Third, the issue of data functionality. DAC is generated for some purpose by someone, and there is always an expected function. There may be a political meaning that can be read into it, or the possibility of modifying it to more effective data functionally. This book takes a critical functionalist stance on DAC which avoids the dichotomy of "correct data/wrong data" as much as possible, and judges the nature of the data from the three perspectives of scientific durability, social credibility, and functionality.

However, this book does not aim to cover all war data and evaluate it from these three perspectives; instead, it aims to present a useful schematic for understanding

---

[29] The following essay was referenced in considering the position of critical functionalism. Elizabeth Pisani and Maarten Kok, "In the Eye of the Beholder: To Make Global Health Estimates Useful, Make Them More Socially Robust," *Global Health Action* 10 (2017).

DAC from these three perspectives. In other words, it aims to provide the minimum prerequisite knowledge necessary for readers to judge the nature of any DAC they receive in the future. This book focuses on the area of "civilian (non-combatant) deaths in war" within DAC and presents a schematic of DAC. Before entering into specific discussions, it explains the basic terms related to DAC and the framework for analysis.

1.2 What is Data on Armed Conflicts?

Clarification of Terms

I have used the term "data on armed conflicts (DAC)" or "war data" many times so far, but we have not sufficiently defined its meaning. At this juncture, it is imperative to organize the fundamental terms presented herein. In this book, "war" is defined as "a social phenomenon in which multiple actors clash using organized and continuous violence to achieve their respective goals, resulting in deaths," while there is also the concept of "armed conflict" besides war. There are views that armed conflict includes phenomena where military force is used outside of war, but in this book, armed conflict and war are used in the same meaning in principle.[30]

What is more important is the word "data." When we say "data on armed conflicts" or "war data" in this book, we use it in the sense of "a bundle of information necessary to explain the nature of a particular war." In this book, we focus on the generation of data related to "civilian (non-combatant) deaths" among DAC: for example, data on the number of civilian deaths in war; the attributes and identities of the deceased; and the cause of death. This is because, after the end of the Cold War, "civilian deaths" have been one of the most important issues in the study and reporting of armed conflicts.[31]

---

[30] To elaborate on the relationship between armed conflict and war. Before World War I, the laws of war targeted wars between nations, but a declaration of war by one of the nations was required as a condition of that war (legal war). A declaration of war refers to, for example, a declaration of the start of war or an ultimatum. If there was no declaration of war, it was considered an act of force that did not lead to war, but after World War I, there were many cases of hostile acts equivalent to war without a declaration of war (de facto war). In order to respond to the situation where legal wars and de facto wars coexist, the concept of "armed conflict" began to be used in international law instead of "war." However, in this book, we use the terms armed conflict and war synonymously, defining war not by the requirement of a declaration of war, but by the nature of hostile acts.

[31] There is a vast amount of prior research on the protection of civilians, for example, Colm McKeogh, *Innocent Civilians: The Morality of Killing in War* (Basingstoke: Palgrave, 2002); Hellen M. Kinsella, *The Image before the Weapon: A Critical History of the Distinction between Combatant and Civilian* (Ithaca, N.Y.: Cornell University Press, 2011); Robert Schütte, *Civilian Protection in Armed Conflicts: Evolution, Challenges and Implementation* (Wiesbaden: Springer VS, 2015); Haidi Willmot et al., eds., *Protection of Civilians* (Oxford: Oxford University Press, 2016); Joe Cropp, *The Humanitarian Fix: Navigating Civilian Protection in Contemporary Wars* (Abingdon: Routledge, 2021), and others.

There are various types of war data, which can be divided into "primary data" and "secondary data." Primary data refers to data obtained as a result of directly collecting information related to war through interviews, forensic investigations, etc. Administrative information collected for entirely different purposes, such as population data from peacetime censuses, is also included in primary data. Primary data is distinguished from secondary data, with the latter referring to information that has been processed and edited from primary data. For example, the results calculated from primary data presented by researchers in papers and similar sources can be mentioned. According to this distinction, the thesis introduced earlier by Kaldor that "80% of war deaths are civilians" was the result of calculations based on secondary data.

One type of secondary data is an "estimate." An estimate is a value derived by collecting primary data from one area for a region where primary data cannot be directly obtained, and applying some form of statistical processing to it. For example, by using pre-war population data, peacetime age-specific mortality rates, and post-war population data, we can derive the population data that could have existed if the war had not occurred, and compare it with the actual post-war population data. This may allow us to estimate the number of people who may have died as a result of the war.

On the battlefield, there are many situations where it is difficult to collect primary data directly. It would be most accurate if we could confirm who died where for each individual, but that is almost impossible. In this case, the focus becomes how to generate the necessary data from the data that already exists. Therefore, in the generation of DAC, an estimate often becomes an essential task. Not only in wars, but also in regions where the infrastructure for information collection is undeveloped or collapsed, such estimates are actively carried out in fields such as public health and hygiene.

Framework of Analysis (1): International Norms

At this point, we should investigate the structure of DAC, beginning with a specific example. In July 2022, the Office of the United Nations High Commissioner for Human Rights (OHCHR) announced that more than 5,000 civilians had died in Ukraine since Russia began its invasion on February 24 of the same year,[32] with various media reporting it. What can we learn from this?

First, we need to consider why it is necessary to count civilian casualties as an independent category. The reason why the UN currently counts and announces the number of civilian casualties is because there is an international norm that civilians should not be unnecessarily killed. The current war data is primarily based on norms established by international humanitarian law. While the specific norms adhered to may vary depending on the entity collecting the data, the international community generally adheres to these standards regarding warfare.

International humanitarian law, which primarily deals with the protection of war victims (Geneva Law) and the regulation of means of harming the enemy (Hague

[32] https://www.ohchr.org/en/news/2022/07/ukraine-civilian-casualty-update-12-july-2022.

Law), is adhered to in the data generated by the United Nations and NGOs. International humanitarian law, born in the nineteenth century, was initially created to improve the treatment of soldiers. During this period, Western countries began to bear the responsibility of explaining to society how soldiers died; therefore, international humanitarian law established rules to prevent the dispersion of information about soldiers' deaths. The international norm of civilian protection, which this book focuses on, was not explicitly formulated until after World War II, and the systematic collection of data on civilian deaths did not begin until even later (these will be analyzed in Chaps. 2 and 3).

In addition, from the late nineteenth century to after World War II, laws concerning the methods of war were called "laws of war" (droit de la guerre), while the term "international humanitarian war" (droit international humanitaire) appeared in the 1960s.[33] In this book, all laws concerning the methods of war are referred to by their current name, international humanitarian war.

If we claim that DAC fundamentally presupposes international humanitarian law, the question arises as to whether there is any war data that does not presuppose it. For example, what about data on the total amount of food consumed by an army in a certain war? This does not seem to be directly related to issues under international humanitarian law (however it may be indirectly related if the army has plundered civilian food). Because of its weak connection with humanitarian law, this data is unlikely to become a point of contention in the international community. Indeed, it is unlikely that the total amount of food consumed by the Russian army in the Ukraine war that broke out in 2022 has been a topic of discussion. The depth of the relationship with humanitarian law is proportional to normative importance. Certainly, exceptions may occur when the provisions of humanitarian law can no longer cover new issues, but this proportional relationship will generally hold.

Analytical Framework (2): Scientific Analysis

Now, there is another point to consider from the previous example: how OHCHR came up with that number. On this point, OHCHR states the following:

> Since 2014, OHCHR has been documenting civilian casualties in Ukraine. Reports are based on information that the UN Human Rights Monitoring Mission in Ukraine (HRMMU) collected through interviews with victims and their relatives; witnesses; analysis of corroborating material confidentially shared with HRMMU; official records; open-source documents, photo and video materials; forensic records and reports; criminal investigation materials; court documents; reports by international and national non-governmental organizations; public reports by law enforcement and military actors; data from medical facilities and local authorities. All sources and information are assessed for their relevance and credibility and cross-checked against other information.[34]

---

[33] Amanda Alexander, "A Short History of International Humanitarian Law," *The European Journal of International Law* 26, no. 1 (2015).

[34] https://www.ohchr.org/en/news/2022/07/ukraine-civilian-casualty-update-12-july-2022.

Thus, in order to prove whether civilian deaths actually occurred on the battlefield, it is necessary to collect and analyze a vast amount of primary and secondary data. The process of deriving specific numbers from data analysis is based on scientific thinking, and behind the specific number of civilian deaths there is a scientific analysis process in addition to international norms. The data utilized by the OHCHR, which I intend to focus on here, comprises forensic records. What is forensic science? This will be discussed in detail in Chap. 6 but, simply put, it is a field of study that collects and analyzes scientific evidence needed for criminal investigations and trials.

The method used by OHCHR to derive the number of civilian casualties in the Ukrainian War, as mentioned earlier, can be called an "adding up method," that is, it is a method of counting each civilian casualty. However, in cases where the war is too large and long-term, this adding up method often does not work; in fact, it is almost impossible to find all the bodies on the battlefield and, therefore, the adding up method may underestimate the number of deaths. In that case, you have to include the dead who have not been found in the numbers, which is where statistical analysis comes in, which can be used to grasp the overall picture of civilian damage. This will be discussed in Chap. 5.

As mentioned above, when generating DAC, it can be seen that reality is observed and analyzed through two filters. The first filter is international norms, which determine what to datafy. The second filter is the scientific process, which generates data that can withstand objective criticism. In this book, we will examine the formation of international norms in the first half and take up some specific scientific analysis processes in the second half. These two cognitive filters are shown in the following diagram (Fig. 1.1).

Sovereign States and Humanitarian Networks

Who generates DAC through these two filters? Various actors are involved. In the case of the Ukrainian War mentioned earlier, OHCHR reported the number of deaths, but in the generation of DAC, sovereign states, international organizations, NGOs, etc. are involved. However, historically, the generation of DAC was the exclusive jurisdiction of sovereign states. After all, it was not until the late nineteenth century that sovereign states began to investigate and datafy the deaths of their own soldiers. The nineteenth century was a time when the Red Cross was born and international humanitarian law developed greatly along with health and sanitation systems in wars, with the idea of soldier welfare taking root in Europe. However, organizations such

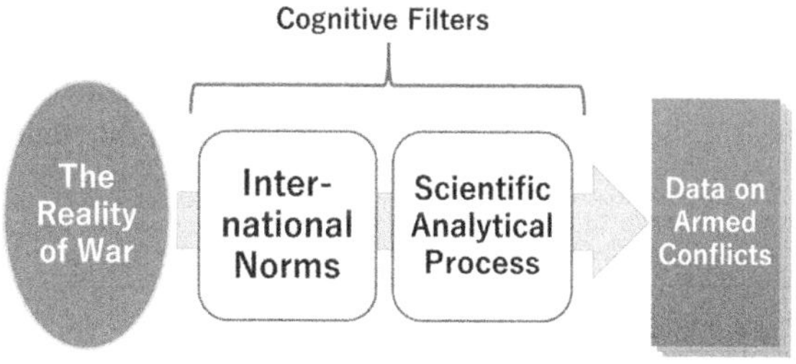

Fig. 1.1 Cognitive filters in DAC generation

as the Red Cross societies of various countries and the International Committee of the Red Cross were essentially born and developed to complement the armies of sovereign states; therefore, they were not generally allowed to release information that would oppose the state. International organizations and NGOs began to get involved in the generation of DAC against states in the latter half of the twentieth century.

The United Nations began to get involved in the generation of DAC gradually from around 1970, starting with investigations into the territories occupied as a result of the Third Arab–Israeli War. Human rights NGOs, with the birth of Amnesty International and Human Rights Watch, began to actively investigate and publish DAC in the 1980s, often cooperating with each other in the generation of DAC and building close relationships with international organizations such as the United Nations. This became a global network for generating DAC.

When international organizations and NGOs began to generate DAC, the DAC published by sovereign states began to be compared and examined with other data. In war, the military (or armed forces) that monopolize military power are overwhelmingly superior compared to civilians. However, there are often cases where states and armed forces do not (or cannot) fully account for their military actions, such as killing soldiers and civilians. In such cases, it is international organizations and human rights NGOs that generate more scientifically durable data, which often serves as a counter to the claims of sovereign states. Citizens who have been oppressed and killed by the military or armed forces are first recognized, and survivors (or bereaved families) claim their violated rights through this counter information.

Thus, DAC itself sometimes becomes a field of political struggle. Who was killed when and how, who violated international humanitarian law when and how; for conflict actors, these questions themselves are related to their legitimacy, so they sometimes react excessively to the investigation reports of international organizations and NGOs. Such struggles have been seen around the world since the end of the Cold War, with the Syrian conflict that broke out in 2011 and the Ukrainian War that broke out in 2022 no exceptions. Therefore, this book mainly focuses on the generation of DAC by international organizations and NGOs, and clarifies how it has been in conflict with states and armed forces.

The mass media is deeply involved in the issue of DAC. In the Crimean War of 1853, which is also called "the first media war in history," journalism that reported on the situation on the battlefield developed due to technological innovations such as telegraphy.[35] As a result, the number and cause of soldier deaths became a significant issue in public opinion in Britain and, subsequently, information technology rapidly developed and the mass media began to disseminate detailed information about the battlefield. The Vietnam War of the 1960s, in which America was mired, is also called the "Living Room War," as the situation on the battlefield was vividly conveyed to

[35] Ulrich Keller, *The Ultimate Spectacle: A Visual History of the Crimean War* (New York: Routledge, 2001), 251.

each household through the spread of television.[36] The American government, in turn, could not hide the serious situation in Vietnam, and American public opinion began to lean towards anti-war sentiments. Furthermore, in the Gulf War of 1991, satellite broadcasts transmitted real-time information to various parts of the world.[37] And with the development of the internet and information devices, from the 2000s onwards, citizens have been able to disseminate information individually, and the micro-details of wars have been exchanged in vast amounts of information.[38]

The number of civilian casualties in wars, which this book focuses on, is regularly announced by the mass media and thus reaches the general public. Certainly, the United Nations and NGOs publish information on their websites, but the number of citizens who directly access this information is very small compared to those who access newspapers, television, and news sites. However, the mass media occupies an indirect position in the generation of DAC; while it is true that newspapers sometimes independently investigate civilian casualties, these efforts are sporadic at best. Comprehensive and long-term investigations of civilian casualties are primarily conducted by international organizations and NGOs.

Characteristics of Humanitarian Networks

The concept of "networks" is important when analyzing data generation by international organizations and NGOs. Even in the case of the United Nations, it does not necessarily have all the scientific expertise needed to generate DAC. The generation of DAC requires a wide range of experts, including forensic scientists (a general term including forensic archaeologists, forensic anthropologists, and forensic pathologists), DNA experts, statisticians, chemists, etc. If legal responsibility for illegal actions is to be pursued, experts in international law are also needed. Therefore, when international organizations and NGOs generate DAC, they use international networks to form teams tailored to their projects and conduct investigations.

The study of sociologist Bruno Latour can be instructive in understanding the characteristics of this network. In his book *Science in Action*, Latour attempted to elucidate the process by which scientists and engineers produce facts and machines, gain many supporters, and eventually become widely accepted as established science. Latour also introduced the concept of "networks" whereby the small number of people who produce facts become visible and influential only by connecting with the

[36] Rodger Streitmatter, *Mightier than the Sword: How the News Media Have Shaped American History* (New York: Routledge, 2018), Ch. 12.

[37] Andrew Hoskins and Ben O'Loughlin, *War and Media: The Emergence of Diffused War* (Cambridge: Polity Press, 2010), 16–17.

[38] P. W. Singer and Emerson T. Brooking, *Likewar: The Weaponization of Social Media* (Boston: Houghton Mifflin Harcourt, 2018).

vast majority of people who are not involved in science. While networks of science and technology are widely diffused, resources are accumulated in only a few places.[39]

The network of experts involved in the generation of DAC also has these characteristics. There are few experts and specialized institutions capable of dealing with large-scale armed conflicts, and they are scattered around the world. Therefore, international organizations and NGOs, including the United Nations, form a network of experts and specialized institutions each time to generate DAC. The generation of DAC by these networks relies on the provisions and purposes of international humanitarian law, which sets rules on the methods of war. In this book, we call these networks for generating DAC "humanitarian networks."

According to Latour's network theory, the more experts connected in a network and more data generated through its routes, the more scientifically durable the data is considered to be. The more scientists review it, the less scientific error there is. However, just because data is scientifically durable does not mean it is socially reliable. International organizations and NGOs need to appeal their data and its interpretation widely to society, separate from data generation, and aim for activities such as policy changes to create social impact. Without gaining political support and funding, they cannot continue to generate data. When various data are mixed and cause controversy, the most scientifically reliable data should become persuasive material. However, in actual controversies, it is not that simple.

*

This book will now analyze the structure of DAC generation. The framework for this analysis is, as mentioned earlier, two cognitive filters (international norms and scientific processes) and two types of actors (sovereign states and humanitarian networks). In Chap. 2, we analyze how the protection of war casualties, essential for the collection of information on the deceased, became an international norm. We also examine how this norm was put into practice. In Chap. 3, we analyze how the protection of civilians became an international norm through a specific historical process. In Chap. 4, we analyze the historical process by which international organizations and NGOs began to collect and publish DAC. In Chap. 5, we examine statistical analysis methods for estimating the total number of war casualties, especially civilian casualties. In Chap. 6, we examine forensic investigations that analyze on a micro level who the casualties were and how they died. In Chap. 7, we focus on chemical weapons among the weapons used in war and examine their use investigation.

[39] Bruno Latour, *Science in Action: How to Follow Scientists and Engineers through Society* (Cambridge: Harvard University Press, 1987), 179–213.

As such, this book covers a wide range of topics related to war, international law, statistics, forensic medicine, and chemical weapons, but it is written to be as understandable as possible for beginners. We have thus avoided overly specialized discussions as much as possible and narrowed the scope to discussions necessary for creating an "overview."

Chapter 2
International Standardization of Combatant Protection

Contents

Abstract This chapter examines the process of establishing international norms for the protection of war casualties. From the 19th to the early 20th century, the protection of war casualties became an international norm in Europe. This was driven by the problem of a large number of missing persons caused by various wars, including the Austro-Prussian War. International conferences were convened on numerous occasions with the objective of enhancing the conduct of warfare in a more humane manner. This resulted in the establishment of regulations pertaining to the protection of bodies and the collection of data on casualties. The International Committee of the Red Cross (ICRC) played a pivotal role in supporting this process of international standardization. During the First World War, practices based on these norms were attempted, yet they did not always yield the desired outcomes. At the outset of the war, states were confronted with the challenge of processing a vast amount of information about missing persons and war casualties. However, their initial processing capacity proved inadequate to the task. Over time, however, their processing capacity improved, and a system was established for states to manage the deaths of their citizens as soldiers.

In the Ukraine War that began in 2022, many soldiers and civilians went missing, and their families have been worried and suffering about the safety of the missing. The International Committee of the Red Cross (ICRC), an NGO based in Geneva, is responsible for collecting information about the missing in war and responding to inquiries from families.[1] The ICRC accepts contacts from citizens of both Russia and

[1] Imogen Foulkes, "Ukraine War: Helping Families Find Missing Loved Ones," BBC, June 26, 2022, https://www.bbc.com/news/world-europe-61926983.

M. Igarashi, *War and Data on Armed Conflicts*, Evidence-Based Approaches to Peace and Conflict Studies 14, https://doi.org/10.1007/978-981-97-6418-1_2

Ukraine in a neutral position. Their activities are recognized and protected by international humanitarian law, which also stipulates a rule that the belligerents protect the deceased (bodies) that occur in armed conflicts.[2] To confirm the information of the missing, this rule to protect the deceased (bodies) is most important. This is because protecting the bodies leads to the accurate creation of a list of war casualties, and confirming the deceased reduces the number of those missing. This chapter examines the historical development and implementation of this norm of casualty protection.[3]

This international norm was first codified in the Convention for the Amelioration of the Condition of the Wounded and Sick in Armies in the Field (hereafter, the Geneva Convention of 1906). The chapter reexamines the process leading to the establishment of the Geneva Convention of 1906 and elucidates how the protection of the war dead was grounded and codified through diplomatic documents and discourses from international legal scholars involved in its international standardization.

The international standardization of the protection of war dead began in Europe in the second half of the nineteenth century. A particularly important turning point was the Austro-Prussian War that broke out in 1866. Until then, in European wars, when lower-ranking soldiers died, they were typically buried in groups without their identities being specified.[4] It was rare for the state to explain the death of a lower-ranking soldier to his family or to bury him with his name clearly stated. Therefore, the cumbersome task of protecting bodies on the battlefield to collect information about the dead and identify them was rarely carried out.

---

[2] Particularly relevant in international humanitarian law are Article 15 (Search and Collection of the Wounded and Sick), Article 16 (Recording and Forwarding of Information), and Article 17 (Registration of the Dead and Graves) of the First Geneva Convention of 1949.

[3] The preceding research on this chapter can be broadly divided into two categories. One is research on the identification of soldiers, including Luc Capdevila and Daniele Voldman, *War Dead: Western Societies and the Casualties of War*, trans. Richard Veasey (Edinburgh: Edinburgh University Press, 2006); Veronique Harouel-Bureloup, "Identifier les corps des militaires morts au combat," in *Revue historique de droit francais et etranger*, no. 3 (Juillet-Septembre 2017); Jan P.P. Ganschow, "Identification of the Fallen: The Supply of "Dog Tags" to Soldiers as a Commandment of the Laws of War," *New Zealand Armed Forces Law Review* 9 (2009), among others. The other is research on the burial methods of bodies, for example, George L. Mosse, *Fallen Soldiers: Reshaping the Memory of the World Wars* (New York: Oxford University Press, 1990); Thomas W. Laqueur, *The Work of the Dead: A Cultural History of Mortal Remains* (Princeton: Princeton University Press, 2015); Simon Harold Walker, *Physical Control, Transformation and Damage in the First World War: War Bodies* (London: Bloomsbury Academic, 2021); Daniel J. Sherman, *The Construction of Memory in Interwar France* (Chicago: The University of Chicago Press, 1999). Further, for research on the burial of Japan's war dead, see Toshio Kurihara, *Remains: Postwar History of the 3.1 Million War Dead* (Tokyo: Iwanami Shoten, 2015) [Japanese]; Kazufumi Hamai, *Postwar History of Overseas War Dead: Repatriation of Remains and Memorialization* (Tokyo: Yoshikawa Kobunkan, 2014) [Japanese]; Emiko Namihira, *Forms of Death in Japan: From Traditional Ceremonies to Yasukuni* (Tokyo: Asahi Shimbunsha, 2004) [Japanese].

[4] Mosse, *Fallen Soldiers*, 44–45; Thomas W. Laqueur, "Memory and Naming in the Great War," in *Commemorations: The Politics of National Identity*, ed. John R. Gillis, 151–52 (Princeton: Princeton University Press, 1994).

However, from the mid-nineteenth century onwards in Europe, a humanitarian idea spread that the pain soldiers suffer in war should be reduced as much as possible, and norms and practices for the protection of wounded and sick on the battlefield developed. Along with this, norms and practices for the protection of the bodies of deceased soldiers, identification of their identities, and explanation to their families also developed, which was gradually codified through several international conferences. This norm did not remain in Europe, but was also accepted and practiced in America and Japan, becoming a truly international norm.

How was such an international norm founded? As this chapter will show, the international norm of the protection of war dead was founded above all on empathy for the pain of soldiers' families. According to international law scholars of the time, in an international society composed of civilized nations, norms of charity and humanity were becoming pervasive with the development of civilization. Based on this charity and humanity, it was considered one of the duties of civilized nations to alleviate the pain of soldiers' families.

2.1 What is Combat Death and Combatant Protection?

Even when we refer to "combat death," we must carefully consider what types of death this term encompasses. On the battlefield, many people lose their lives due to physical attacks associated with combat. This is a "biological death," however, this does not necessarily mean a "social death." In other words, unless the people who knew the deceased recognize his/her death, he/she is not considered socially dead.

However, soldiers cannot assert their own identity from the moment they become corpses. Therefore, the identity of this deceased soldier can only be determined through active investigation by other soldiers or humanitarian activists. Without such investigations, the state cannot grasp who among its citizens has died as a soldier, and the bereaved families, far away from the battlefield, cannot know the fact that their loved ones have died. In this way, soldiers who have lost their lives in war die socially only after a biological death and an investigation of the body. Both biological and social deaths are included in combat death.

If a soldier has biologically died but has not died socially, the remaining family will continue to worry about the soldier's safety. In recent years, this distress has been called "ambiguous loss" and has been the subject of analysis and treatment. "Ambiguous loss is inherently traumatic because the inability to resolve the situation causes pain, confusion, shock, distress, and often immobilization."[5] The concept of "ambiguous loss" was born from research on families of soldiers who went missing in the Vietnam War,[6] but this mental state itself has been tormenting many families long before that.

---

[5] Pauline Boss, *Loss, Trauma, and Resilience: Therapeutic Work with Ambiguous Loss* [Ebook] (New York: W. W. Norton, 2006), 18.

[6] Ibid., 22.

Protection of Bodies and Collection of Identity Information

Unfortunately, it is often extremely difficult to identify the deceased during a war. What is needed is the protection of the deceased, but to clarify this, we need to consider how biological death occurs in the first place. The situations in which a soldier loses his life can be classified as follows:

(A) Death on the battlefield (buried on the spot or left as is).
(B) Detained by the enemy's army as a prisoner of war and died for some reason.
(C) Admitted to a medical facility of one's own army as a wounded or sick person and died.
(D) Died for some reason (such as suicide) unrelated to combat.

In actual wars, the extent to which each belligerent recognizes "combat death" varies depending on the policy of the country, but here we will confirm the difficulties in identifying the deceased associated with (A) to (C), which are generally classified as combat deaths.

Firstly, when a soldier dies on the battlefield, it is often difficult to immediately identify the body due to the ongoing combat. It is fortunate if the military can quickly and accurately grasp the fact that a soldier has died, but there are many cases where it is completely impossible to understand who died, when, and how, such as when a unit is annihilated. In such cases, bodies are collected after the battle ends, identification is carried out, and data related to the soldier's death is generated.

However, if the body does not possess any belongings that indicate its identity, this task becomes extremely difficult, or the body may be buried without any markers. Furthermore, it is conceivable that the body may be severely damaged by explosions during combat, making it impossible to perform an autopsy. To avoid these problems as much as possible, it is necessary to supply dog tags that clearly state the soldier's identity, protect the body and belongings, and record the burial location.

If a soldier dies while being detained as a prisoner of war in enemy military facilities, the soldier's death information will certainly exist if the enemy army knows the prisoner's identity; the issue is whether or not to send the prisoner's information to the opposing country. In this case, the point of contention is whether or not it is possible to exchange prisoner information between warring countries. If a soldier dies in a military medical facility in their own country due to injury or illness, it becomes easier to collect information, but if the information is not successfully sent from the hospital to the military, and then from the military to the bereaved family, the deceased soldier cannot socially die.

When a biological death occurs in this way, if the body and belongings are not actively and appropriately protected on the battlefield, in prisoner of war camps, or in military hospitals, and if the identity is not investigated, it is impossible to reach a social death. This is why the norm of protecting the dead in war was born. Protection of the war dead means the protection of bodies that have occurred in war and the collection of identity information.

The generation of data on war casualties began with the development of this war dead protection norm. Who, where, when, and how did they die? The state collects this information and explains it to the bereaved family. In the process, bundles of DAC have been generated. Therefore, when examining the history of the generation of DAC, it is inevitable to focus on the history of war dead protection.

2.2 The Beginning of International Standardization of Combatant Protection

Until the Establishment of the Geneva Convention in 1864

How was the protection of the war dead internationalized? The protection of the war dead was advocated as part of international humanitarian law and has permeated. Therefore, it is necessary to first examine how the movement to codify international humanitarian law began.

The Red Cross, with its founder Henri Dunant, supported the development of international humanitarian law.[7] Born in Geneva in 1828, Dunant began working at a bank in Geneva at the age of eighteen and traveled to Algeria and Tunisia for about two years from the age of twenty-five. When he turned thirty, he set up a milling company in Algeria, which was a French colony at the time, but he could not solve the problem of water needed for the farmland, so he decided to directly petition Emperor Napoleon III of France. On his journey, he encountered the Second Italian War of Independence that broke out in 1859.

This war was caused by the Kingdom of Sardinia's aim to unify the Italian peninsula.[8] At that time, Austria held dominion over the Italian peninsula, so the Kingdom of Sardinia sought the possibility of unifying Italy by having France fight Austria. Therefore, in the Crimean War that broke out in 1853, the Kingdom of Sardinia lent troops to the French army and built a relationship with France. Subsequently, as France also wanted to weaken Austria, the Kingdom of Sardinia finally decided to wage war against Austria with France.

The fierce battleground was Solferino, located about 150 km west of Venice. In a village near Solferino called Castiglione, Dunant encountered a large number of wounded soldiers and the villagers who were helping them. Dunant, forgetting his original purpose of the journey, worked hard with the villagers to aid the wounded, with his experiences there depicted in his book *A Memory of Solferino* (1862). He wrote about the handling of the bodies of the dead as follows:

> In the French Army a certain number of soldiers were detailed from each company to identify and bury the dead. Usually they picked out the men of their own units. They took the regimental number on the dead man's belongings, and then, with the help of Lombard peasants paid for the purpose, laid the body, clothed, in a common grave. Unhappily, in their

---

[7] For the early history of the Red Cross, including Dunant, see Pierre Boissier, *From Solferino to Tsushima: History of the International Committee of the Red Cross* (Geneva: Henry Dunant Institute, 1985), Ch. 2 and 3; James Crossland, *War, Law and Humanity: The Campaign to Control Warfare, 1853–1914* (London: Bloomsbury, 2018), Ch. 4.

[8] Geoffrey Wawro, *Warfare and Society in Europe, 1792–1914* (Abingdon: Routledge, 2000), 65–71.

> haste to finish their work, and because of the carelessness and gross negligence of some of the peasants, there is every reason to believe that more than one live man was buried with the dead. The decorations, money, watches, letters and papers found on the officers were later sent to their families; but it was not always possible to fulfill this duty properly, with such a vast number of bodies to be buried.[9]

The most important thing in handling bodies at that time was to prevent the spread of infectious diseases through the bodies. Therefore, it was necessary to bury the bodies in the ground as soon as possible. In the case of officers, measures were taken to respect individual identities, such as sending personal belongings to their families, but for ordinary soldiers, they were simply buried in a common grave, and there was little effort to identify or respect individual identities.

At the end of this book, Dunant proposed an international agreement on organizations to aid wounded soldiers, which led to the establishment of the first Geneva Convention two years later. This Geneva Convention consisted of ten articles, including the neutrality of those who provide aid on the battlefield. The purpose of this convention was to ensure the safety of aid workers and create a humanitarian space where the wounded and sick could be reliably treated. From this period, aid societies, later known as the Red Cross, were established in various countries, becoming the most famous humanitarian organization in the world.

The establishment and subsequent development of this Geneva Convention was supported by the "Committee of Five" in Geneva, later known as the International Committee of the Red Cross (ICRC). The five were Henri Dunant, physician Théodore Maunoir, physician Louis Appia, military officer Henri Dufour, and lawyer Gustave Moynier. In particular, Moynier continued to disseminate a concrete vision of international humanitarian law until the establishment of the Geneva Convention in 1906.

It is important to note that the ICRC and the Red Cross societies of each country are different organizations. The ICRC is a non-governmental organization based in Geneva, Switzerland, which promoted the codification of international humanitarian law and conducted activities at an international level. The Red Cross societies of each country were recognized in their respective countries, often received public financial aid, and had a function to supplement their own military forces in wars.

2.3 Austro-Prussian War

The Geneva Convention of 1864 was first practiced on the battlefield in the Austro-Prussian War of 1866. At that time, Prussia was aiming for the unification of Germany, but Austria stood in the way. Austria had established a leading position in this region and wanted to maintain it as well as the status quo in order to suppress the nationalism of each ethnic group.[10] In 1866, they finally came to a military conflict, but before

[9] Henry Dunant, *A Memory of Solferino* (Geneve: ICRC, 1959), 49.

[10] Wawro, *Warfare and Society in Europe*, 84–91.

the war, Austria was seen as having the advantage. However, in reality, the Prussian army outmaneuvered the Austrian army, and the victory of the former was decided in less than two months, which is why the war is also called the Seven Weeks' War.

In this war, the Prussian side actively endeavored to fulfill the Geneva Convention. Medical personnel and military clergy wore Red Cross armbands and aided wounded soldiers on both sides. However, the Austrian side, which had not signed the Geneva Convention, showed little attitude to fulfill it. On the contrary, the Austrian army often took all of its medical personnel with them when they retreated, leaving behind field hospitals and the wounded soldiers housed there. As a result, many soldiers who could have survived if treated lost their lives.[11]

Thus, the Austrian army produced a large number of casualties, but at the same time, it had to deal with a large number of missing persons. According to Austrian historian Gaston Bodart, the number of dead on the Austrian side exceeded 7000, and the number of missing persons approached 12,000,[12] which served as a wake-up call to the Austrian military and government officials about the importance of protecting the dead in war.

The First International Red Cross Conference (Paris International Conference)

The first time the protection of the war dead was explicitly discussed was at the First International Red Cross Conference, held in Paris in August 1867, where Red Cross societies from various countries gathered.[13] This year, International Exposition was held in Paris, and the Red Cross was also scheduled to exhibit there, so an international conference on battlefield relief was held to coincide with it.[14] The conference was attended by representatives from 17 countries, mainly in Europe, including Austria, Belgium, Spain, America, France, Britain, Italy, the Netherlands, Portugal, Prussia, Russia, and Turkey. The representatives included members of each country's aid societies, as well as government officials and international law scholars.[15]

The main points of discussion at the conference were warfare at sea, which was not covered by the 1864 Geneva Convention, maintaining law and order on the battlefield after combat, soldiers' identification tags, and the exchange of lists of prisoners of war. All of these points, except for warfare at sea, were related to the protection of the war dead. At that time, there were people who looted soldiers' equipment indiscriminately from the dead and survivors after the battle.[16] As a result, not only

---

[11] Boissier, *From Solferino to Tsushima*, 183–84.

[12] Gaston Bodart, *Losses of Life in Modern Wars: Austria-Hungary; France*, ed. Harold Westergaard (Oxford: The Clarendon Press, 1916), 58.

[13] At that time, this conference was not called "the International Conference of the Red Cross." The minutes are recorded as "Conférences internationales à Paris."

[14] Boissier, *From Solferino to Tsushima*, 199.

[15] The Red Cross societies of each country were still called by their respective names, and there was no common name of "Red Cross Society." Here, to avoid confusion of names, they are referred to as "aid societies."

[16] Gustave Moynier, *Etude sur la Convention de Genève pour l'amélioration du sort des militaires blessés dans les armées en campagne, 1864 et 1868* (New York: Kessinger Publishing, 2010[1870]), 272–75.

were survivors in danger, but they often lost their belongings and the identities of the bodies became unknown. Sometimes even the bodies were damaged. Therefore, it was necessary to maintain law and order on the battlefield after combat to protect not only survivors but also the war dead. Also, to more effectively identify the bodies, it was important to introduce identification tags that clearly stated the soldier's personal information.[17] Furthermore, for the safety investigation of missing persons, it is essential to exchange lists of prisoners, deceased, etc., which is deeply related to the generation of casualty data.

What was the discussion at the actual conference? On August 27, one of the five committee members, Moynier, chaired a discussion on the issues related to Article 5 of the 1864 Geneva Convention (rescue of the wounded and sick by civilians living near the battlefield). At this point, the Austrian representative introduced the discussion at the Würzburg Conference, which took place prior to this international conference.[18] The Würzburg Conference referred to a meeting on August 22, 1867, where representatives of various aid societies active in the Austro-Prussian War discussed the nature of the Geneva Convention based on their experiences.[19]

At the Würzburg Conference, a revision of the Geneva Convention was created, and Article 5 of this revision was introduced at this point, which stated, "The victorious army has the duty, to the extent that circumstances permit, to militarily oversee the dead and wounded on the battlefield, in order to preserve them from looting and mistreatment."[20] As mentioned earlier, looting after the end of battles was a major issue in wars at the time, and it was necessary to maintain surveillance and public order to prevent it.

Furthermore, the Austrian representative read a document from the Ministry of War and expressed the sentiment that in war, it is necessary to identify the dead as much as possible, regardless of friend or foe, and to oversee burials in accordance with the principles of maintaining sanitary conditions.[21] However, in war, it is often difficult to confirm the status of soldiers. For example, in the Austro-Prussian War, eight months after the end of the battle, 84 officers and 12,277 non-commissioned officers and soldiers in the Austrian army were missing. With the occurrence of this large number of missing persons, the Austrian representative pointed out the following problems:

> Imagine the double misery that families must feel as a result of the uncertainty in which they are plunged regarding the fate of their loved ones, and the unfortunate legal consequences that this uncertainty entails. [...] Thousands of families are suffering from this very issue today. The Ministry of War has just taken serious steps to address the question of how to

---

[17] Ibid., 280–82.

[18] *Conférences internationales à Paris. Sociétés de secours aux blessés militaires des armées de terre et de mer. Tenues à Paris en 1867* (Paris: General Commission of Delegates and Baillière & Sons Printing), 89.

[19] Boissier, *From Solferino to Tsushima*, 209.

[20] Moynier, *Study on the Geneva Convention*, 114.

[21] *Conférences internationales à Paris*, 90–94.

eliminate this inconvenience, and it is convinced that with goodwill, the problem can be resolved.[22]

Thus, the safety of the soldiers who had gone to war was uncertain, causing great distress and suffering for their families. Needless to say, families hope that their loved ones who have gone to war are alive. However, after the war is over, if they do not return home and there is no news, it becomes difficult for them to believe in the survival of the soldiers, and they fall into a very unstable psychological state where they cannot even conclude that they are dead. Unfortunately, due to the outbreak of World War I about half a century later, families all over Europe would experience this suffering.

What is noteworthy here is that the interest in the death of soldiers is stronger than in previous wars. As historian George Mosse says, "After the Prussian-Austrian War of 1866 the common soldier's status was upgraded, and his name began to be listed on the war monuments themselves on occasion."[23] It is thought that the increase in sympathy for the remaining families may coincide with this change.[24]

Based on the above, the Austrian representative proposed at the conference that in war, the victorious side should first search and monitor the battlefield after the battle through the patrol of the military police. They should collect the bodies and gather as much identification as possible and then, using that identification as a clue, create a list of the deceased with their names and ranks. He mentioned that the Austrian army decided to equip soldiers with notebooks as identification.[25]

At the next day's meeting, discussions were held in earnest about the exchange of prisoner lists and the identification of bodies. The Austrian representative continued to argue that the list of the dead and prisoners should be sent by the military leaders as much as possible. Considering Austria's experience, he stated that it is more painful for families when the situation of the soldiers is uncertain than when it is certain, and used the pain of the families as the basis for his proposal. He then called for the adoption of the clauses proposed at the aforementioned Würzburg conference. He also proposed making it mandatory for soldiers to carry identification notebooks or metal plates.

In response, the Italian representative suggested that if there were many casualties, it would be impossible to identify individuals with just a roster, so something like a metal plate to hang around the neck would be necessary.[26] The necessity of identification tags was recognized by other countries, but it was also suggested that the

---

[22] Ibid., 91.

[23] Mosse, *Fallen Soldiers*, 47.

[24] In Japan, during the period of World War II, a "system of memorializing the war dead" was established, and it was structured to honor the war dead and lead to further mobilization (Tadatoshi Fujii, *Soldiers' War* (Tokyo: Asahi Shimbun Publications, 2019) [Japanese], 248–55. Considering this, how the individualization of war deaths in Europe was related to military mobilization would be an important point of discussion.

[25] *Conférences internationales à Paris*, 91–93.

[26] Ibid., 133–34.

form should not be determined by international agreement, and rather by the judgment of each government. In the end, nothing was decided about the identification tags. However, from the experience of the Austro-Prussian War, it was agreed that it would be impossible to identify the bodies of even the lowest-ranking soldiers without identification tags.[27] It was not mentioned at this meeting, but Prussia supplied its soldiers with metal plate identification tags in the Austro-Prussian War. However, due to superstitions and other reasons, the soldiers often discarded them, and the identification tags did not always function adequately.[28] Prussia then moved towards making the wearing of identification tags mandatory for soldiers.

Finally, Chairman Moynier presented a specific Article 8 proposal. This draft stipulated that each military force should equip each soldier with a unified identification tag to confirm the soldier's identity, with it proposed to include the name, place of birth, and unit of affiliation. In the event of a soldier's death, the identification tag would be collected before burial and sent to the government or military of the country where the soldier was born. It also stipulated that lists of the dead, wounded, sick, and prisoners of war should be sent to the enemy's military forces as soon as possible after combat.[29] This Article 8 proposal was unanimously adopted in the end.

Thus, at the first International Red Cross Conference, the codification of the norms for the protection of the dead was proposed as a specific article and unanimously adopted. However, this was not a formal diplomatic conference to revise the 1864 Geneva Convention, but a conference to consider amendments. Therefore, codification had to wait for further diplomatic conferences. However, several international conferences were held in Geneva and Berlin, and additional provisions to the Geneva Convention were adopted, but the norms for the protection of the dead were not codified.[30]

2.4 From Practice of Combatant Protection to Codification

Franco-German War

The explicit codification of the protection of the war dead was finally established in the Geneva Convention of 1906. Up until that point, several wars had taken place, during which the practice of protecting the war dead had been accumulated. The Geneva Convention of 1906 reflected these accumulated practices. Specifically, these

---

[27] Ibid., 134–35.

[28] Ganschow, "Identification of the Fallen," 30; Sarah I. Ashbridge and David O'Mara, "The *Erkennungsmarke*: The Humanitarian Duty to Identify Fallen German Soldiers 1866–1918," *Journal of Conflict Archaeology* 15, no. 3 (2020): 194; Sarah I. Ashbridge and Simon Verdegem, "Identity Discs: The Recovery and Identification of First World War Soldiers Located during Archaeological Works on the Former Western Front," *Forensic Science International* 317 (2020): 2–3.

[29] *International Conferences in Paris*, 137.

[30] Harouel-Bureloup, "Identifier les corps des militaires morts au combat," 379–82.

were the Franco-German War (1870–71), the American Civil War (1861–65), the Spanish-American War (1898), and the Russo-Japanese War (1904–05).

We should briefly examine the practices of protecting the war dead prior to the 1906 international conference, during which the Geneva Convention was newly drafted. After its victory in the Austro-Prussian War, Prussia was finally aiming for German unification. The next obstacle was France under the rule of Napoleon III. The conflict between Prussia and France would ultimately be resolved by war, but the direct trigger was the dispute between the two countries over the Spanish succession. When Napoleon III insisted to Wilhelm I of Prussia not to intervene permanently in the Spanish succession issue, Bismarck advised Wilhelm I to ignore this claim, successfully provoking France. In July 1870, France declared war on Prussia, and the war broke out.[31] In fact, Prussia fought as the German Army, by involving the southern German states such as Bavaria in the front line.

At this time, there was a significant difference in the relief system between France and Prussia. The Prussian aid society wore the Red Cross armband and tried to demonstrate its neutrality. In addition, while proclaiming neutrality, the aid society, learning from the lessons of the Austro-Prussian War, promoted integration with the Prussian army for relief activities, which established a system where relief activities could be carried out in coordination with the army on the battlefield.[32] This is where the phenomenon of "Red Cross Patriotism," as John Hutchinson puts it, or the militarization of charity, occurred.[33]

In contrast to Prussia, while France did possess an aid society, it lacked adequate preparedness to address the exigencies of a large-scale conflict such as the Franco-German War. There were no wartime relief plans or necessary funds, and no cooperative relationship with the military had been established.[34] Furthermore, unlike Prussia, the French army showed no interest in the Geneva Convention itself. However, when Prussia invaded France, French citizens abused the Red Cross armbands and symbols in an attempt to protect themselves, appealing to Article 5 of the Geneva Convention, which stipulates the protection of residents who care for the wounded.[35] Thus, the French army and aid society were unable to cope with a large number of casualties when the fighting intensified. According to military historian Michael Clodfelter, during the approximately ten months of war, the number of deaths on the German side was 44,781, all military personnel, while on the French side it totaled 138,871.[36]

Furthermore, there was a difference in the identification tags of soldiers. The Prussian army, reflecting on the Austro-Prussian War, made it mandatory for soldiers

---

[31] Wawro, *Warfare and Society in Europe*, 101–07.

[32] John F. Hutchinson, *Champions of Charity: War and the Rise of the Red Cross* (Oxford: Westview Press, 1996), 117–21; Boissier, *From Solferino to Tsushima*, 247.

[33] Hutchinson, *Champions of Charity*, 256.

[34] Hutchinson, *Champions of Charity*, 109–17; Boissier, *From Solferino to Tsushima*, 247.

[35] Boissier, *From Solferino to Tsushima*, 251–52.

[36] Michael Clodfelter, *Warfare and Armed Conflicts: A Statistical Reference to Casualty and Other Figures, 1500–2000* (London: McFarland, 2002), 210–11.

to wear metal identification tags and made efforts to enable identification. Some countries on the German side other than Prussia also supplied identification tags, however, the French army did not supply identification tags, which led to a major problem in identifying the large number of casualties. In the end, it was not until 1881 that France decided to have soldiers carry metal identification tags.[37]

With a large number of casualties, a large number of prisoners of war were also generated. The difference between a family member who went to war being killed or being held as a prisoner of war is naturally significant. However, the exchange of information such as prisoners of war between hostile nations was not easy, which is where the International Committee of the Red Cross (ICRC) came in. As of July 1870, when the declaration of war was made, the ICRC was preparing to collect information on prisoners of war and others,[38] with it having been already decided at the second International Red Cross Conference held in Berlin in 1869 that the ICRC would be responsible for such information collection.[39] As the war progressed, soldiers detained by the enemy army strongly desired to inform their families of their safety, and the ICRC began to mediate the exchange of letters between soldiers.[40] The ICRC also attempted to mediate the exchange of patient and death registers held by each army, however, due to the underdevelopment of the French aid society, the delivery of the hospital admission list from France was not readily implemented.[41] Similarly, while many German soldiers had identification tags, the French side did not mandate the possession of such tags. As a result, the German side had difficulty identifying the bodies of French soldiers, limiting the creation of a death register.[42]

The Franco-German War did not progress as expected in terms of protecting the deceased, but through this war a significant change occurred in the relationship between burial and the state because the state took on the responsibility of burying deceased soldiers. Bodies buried on battlefields or in communal graves were often reassembled into a single ossuary, often accompanied by a memorial monument.[43] Also, agreements between nations regarding burial were made. The Franco-German War eventually ended with the Treaty of Frankfurt, and Article 16 of the treaty

---

[37] Luc Capdevila and Daniéle Voldman, "Du numéro matricule au code génétique: la manipulation du corps des tués de la guerre en quête d'identité," *Revue internationale de la Croix-Rouge* 84, no. 848 (2002): 756–57.

[38] Boissier, *From Solferino to Tsushima*, 263.

[39] Isabelle Vonèche Cardia, "The International Committee of the Red Cross: Identifying the Dead and Tracing Missing Persons – A Historical Perspective," in *Violence, Statistics, and the Politics of Accounting for the Dead*,ed. Marc-Antoine Pérouse de Montclos, Elizabeth Minor, and Samrat Sinha (Wiesbaden: Springer VS, 2015), 74.

[40] Boissier, *From Solferino to Tsushima*, 264; Vonèche Cardia, "The International Committee of the Red Cross," 75.

[41] Boissier, *From Solferino to Tsushima*, 265.

[42] Vonèche Cardia, "The International Committee of the Red Cross," 75.

[43] Guy Flucher, "Modes et lieux d'inhumation, du champ de bataille aux nécropoles nationales," in *Le soldat et la mort dans la Grande Guerre*, dir. Isabelle Homer et Emmanuel Pénicaut (Rennes, 2016), 114.

explicitly stated that France and Germany agreed to respect and maintain the graves of soldiers buried in each other's territories.[44]

The American Civil War and the Spanish–American War

Nine years before the outbreak of the Franco-German War, in 1861, the United States was divided into the Union and Confederate armies, and during this civil war, some protection of the war dead was implemented. In this war, more than 600,000 people lost their lives in both the Union and Confederate armies (including deaths from disease and accidents on the battlefield).[45] Therefore, the protection of the war dead was a significant issue for both armies. Here, we will focus on the Union Army, where the system for protecting the war dead was more developed. About five months after the start of the war, the Union Army issued General Order No. 75, which established a system for creating records of the war dead in all hospitals, and the responsibility for burying deceased soldiers and submitting death records was added to the duties of each army commander.[46] However, this alone was not enough to handle the processing of the bodies and their information due to the large number of war dead.

In April 1862, General Order No. 33 was issued, which provided more detailed instructions. This order more specifically defined the responsibilities of unit commanders for burials. Specifically, it included the surveying of potential burial sites, the requirement to inscribe the numbers and names of the deceased on tombstones, and the recording of tombstone information.[47] Ultimately, in the Union Army, "Of the total interred by 1879, there were 172,109 positive identifications and 143,446 unknown dead."[48] Thus, in the Civil War, it was considered no longer permissible for the state to be indifferent to the war dead.[49]

Certainly, in this war as well, numerous families sought information regarding the well-being and safety of the soldiers deployed to the battlefield. To meet this demand, newspapers in the North and South published lists of the war dead, with the sources of these lists information collected by military chaplains and information provided by officers.[50] When the information provided by the military or government was insufficient, volunteer organizations filled the gap,[51] who investigated and recorded the identities and burial sites of the war dead, and eventually published this

---

[44] Karine Varley, "Under the Shadow of Defeat: The State and the Commemoration of the Franco-Prussian War, 1871–1914," *French History* 16, no. 3 (September 2002).

[45] Clodfelter, *Warfare and Armed Conflicts*, 331.

[46] General Orders No. 75 (September 11, 1861); Edward Steere, *The Graves Registration Service in World War II* (Washington, D.C.: U.S. G.P.O., 1951), 3.

[47] General Orders No. 33 (April 3, 1862); Steere, *The Graves Registration Service*, 4–5.

[48] Steere, *The Graves Registration Service*, 9.

[49] Ibid.

[50] Drew Gilpin Faust, *This Republic of Suffering: Death and the American Civil War* (New York: Alfred A. Knopf, 2008), 103–106.

[51] Ibid., 107–108.

information.[52] Around the same time that Prussia began introducing identification tags, soldiers in the American Civil War also started making and wearing their own name tags. There was no uniform style, and they ranged from metal to cloth. This was the only way to convey information to their families in case they died. In the end, no army officially issued identification tags, but sutlers and local merchants made and sold name tags instead.[53] The US military did not fully introduce identification tags until World War I.

The US military's system for managing war dead evolved significantly during the Spanish-American War, which broke out more than thirty years after the Civil War. This war was a dispute over spheres of influence in the Caribbean and elsewhere between Spain and the United States, with battles taking place in Cuba, Puerto Rico, and the Philippines, among others. Ultimately, more than 3,000 soldiers lost their lives in this war, at least half of whom died from disease.[54] By the end of June 1899, 1222 bodies had been repatriated to the United States, with the unidentified bodies accounting for about 13.63% of the total.[55] The person who directed the handling of the bodies of the war dead in this war was Charles C. Pierce, a military chaplain, who would also contribute to the establishment of a burial record system in World War I. After the Spanish-American War, Pierce was quick to advocate the necessity of identification tags to the military, which would later be adopted by the US military.[56]

Russo–Japanese War

The protection of the war dead was also practiced in the Russo-Japanese War, which broke out in 1904. In this war, the Japanese military tried to adhere as faithfully as possible to the Western norms for the protection of the war dead. Behind this effort was an international political motive that Japan had to diligently comply with international humanitarian law and strive to publicize it in order to demonstrate to the Western powers that it was a country that met the "standards of civilization."[57]

Japan had already established the Philanthropic Society during the Satsuma Rebellion in 1877 and joined the Geneva Convention in 1886 (the following year, the Philanthropic Society was renamed the Japanese Red Cross Society). Furthermore, in 1899, the Hague Land Warfare Convention was established, and Japan ratified it the following year.[58] Thus, in the Russo-Japanese War, the Geneva Convention and the

---

[52] Ibid., 109–10.

[53] Ibid., 120–21. For identification tags in the American Civil War, see Larry B. Maier and Joseph W. Stahl, *Identification Discs of Union Soldiers in the Civil War* (Jefferson: McFarland & Co., Publishers, 2008).

[54] Clodfelter, *Warfare and Armed Conflicts*, 287.

[55] Steere, *The Graves Registration Service*, 10.

[56] Ibid., 10–11.

[57] Naoko Shimazu, *Japanese Society at War: Death, Memory and the Russo-Japanese War* (Cambridge: Cambridge University Press, 2009), 167–76.

[58] For the history of the Japanese Red Cross Society, see Nobuko Kosuge, *Japanese Red Cross Society and the Imperial Household: Philanthropy or Patriotism?* (Tokyo: Yoshikawa Kobunkan, 2021) [Japanese]; Ryuko Yoshikawa, *Founder of the Japanese Red Cross Society: Tsunetami Sano* (Tokyo: Yoshikawa Kobunkan, 2001) [Japanese].

Hague Land Warfare Convention were the main international laws to be applied, but the norms for the protection of the war dead had not yet been codified at this point. Nevertheless, Japan strove to practice as much as possible the norms regarding the protection of the war dead, which had not yet been codified, in order to demonstrate that it was a civilized country.

At that time, the person who worked hard to permeate the understanding of international humanitarian law in the Japanese military was the international law scholar Nagao Ariga. He had been teaching international public law at the Army War College and other institutions since before the Sino-Japanese War, and his students, who went on to serve in the military, had a significant impact on the practice of international law.[59] Ariga served as a legal advisor to the military command during the Sino-Japanese War.[60] In 1896, after returning to Japan, his book *Nisshin Seneki Kokusaihōron* (International Law on the Sino-Japanese War) was published in both Japan and France. In it, Ariga pointed out that it is a civilized country's custom to handle the bodies of the war dead without distinguishing between friend and foe.[61] He also stated that according to international norms, one should ideally perform autopsies on the bodies of enemy soldiers, create a list of the dead, and send it to the enemy side.[62] However, he noted that at the scene of the Sino-Japanese War, while the bodies of Japanese soldiers could be dealt with, they were unable to fully handle the bodies on the Qing side.[63] Although it is a separate issue from the protection of the war dead, the Japanese army was criticized for the Port Arthur incident, where they killed prisoners of war and civilians during this war.

Ariga also served as a legal advisor during the Russo-Japanese War and, after returning to Japan, he published his book *Nichiro Rikusen Kokusaihōron* (International Law on the Russo-Japanese Land War) in both Japanese and French. Even during this war, there was still no codified law regarding the protection of the war dead, but he stated that the norm of protecting the war dead is a "principle of land warfare in the civilized world," and the Japanese army tried to comply with this as much as possible.[64] What is noteworthy is his description regarding the investigation of the deceased's identity, with the Japanese army appearing to have made more efforts to protect the war dead than during the Sino-Japanese War. According to Ariga, under international law at the time, there was an absolute obligation to notify the identity information of those who died after becoming prisoners of war, but there was no absolute obligation for deaths on the battlefield. However, the Japanese government stipulated in Articles 3 and 19 of the Battlefield Cleaning and

[59] Sachiko Matsushita, "Dissemination of International Law in the Russo-Japanese War: Starting with Nagao Ariga" [Japanese], *Military History Studies* 40, no. 2–3 (2004): 195–210.

[60] Sachiko Matsushita, "Nagao Ariga's Experience in Foreign Wars and "Humanitarianism" - During the Sino-Japanese and Russo-Japanese War Periods" [Japanese], *Annual Report of Modern History Research*, no. 5 (March 2013): 6.

[61] Nagao Ariga, *Nisshin Seneki Kokusaihōron* (Rikugun Daigakkō, 1896), 127.

[62] Ibid., 132.

[63] Ibid., 129–31.

[64] Nagao Ariga, *Nichiro Rikusen Kokusaihōron* (Tōkyō Kaikōsha, 1911), 256.

War Dead Burial Regulations (May 30, 1904) that they would also conduct identity investigations for those who died on the battlefield. The Japanese Prisoner of War Information Bureau, in addition to its duties regarding prisoners of war, also collected information about enemies who died on the battlefield and tried to notify the enemy army.[65] Naoko Shimazu, who analyzed Japanese society during the Russo-Japanese War, names this humanitarian practice of Japan, which was mixed with nationalism, "humanitarian nationalism."[66]

Thus, by the turn of the twentieth century, the protection of war dead was becoming established as an international norm among Western powers, and Japan accepted and practiced it as much as possible, promoting it to the major powers. This contributed to the reproduction of the norm of protection of the war dead. As will be discussed next, the experiences from the Russo-Japanese War would be introduced at the diplomatic conference in 1906. However, Japan would later commit large-scale violations of international law during World War II, such as mistreatment of prisoners of war, human experimentation, and executions, often attempting to conceal information about the deaths of prisoners of war.[67]

The Geneva Conference of 1906

In 1906, a diplomatic conference was finally held to revise the Geneva Convention of 1864.[68] The codification of the protection of the war dead was discussed in the first committee, but what to focus on here is the second meeting on June 14, 1906. At this meeting, several specific drafts were presented regarding the clause on the protection of the war dead after combat. The Dutch representative proposed the clause,

> It is the duty of every authority, as well as every military personnel, to protect the wounded and the dead from the enemy against mistreatment, pillaging, and outrage. It is forbidden to use the wounded as a shield against gunfire in combat.[69]

Also, the German representative proposed the clause,

> After the battle, the troops occupying the battlefield will ensure that the wounded are collected, as much as possible, in order to also protect them from looting.[70]

Furthermore, the Austrian representative added a sentence about the identification of the dead,

---

[65] Ibid., 287–95.

[66] Shimazu, *Japanese Society at War*, 169.

[67] Edward Steere and Thayer M. Boardman, *Final Disposition of World War II Dead 1945–1951* (Washington D.C.: Office of the Quartermaster General, 1957), 460–62.

[68] In 1903 and 1904, the ICRC attempted to hold diplomatic conferences twice, but they were unable to realize them due to several reasons, including the outbreak of the Russo-Japanese War (Bossier, *From Solferino to Tsushima*, 373–74).

[69] *Actes de la Conférence de Révision réunie à Genève du 11 juin au 6 juillet 1906* (Genève: Imprimerie H. Jarrys, 1906), 70.

[70] Ibid., 71.

> [Each belligerent who occupies a battlefield] will have to verify the identity of the deceased, ensure regular autopsies, and guarantee burial or cremation in accordance with hygienic requirements.[71]

After discussion, all representatives unanimously accepted the principle of prohibiting the mistreatment and pillaging of the wounded, sick, and dead. The point of contention was whether to include the phrase "as much as possible," but this was resolved by a vote to establish only the principle without this phrase.[72] At the third meeting held two days later, the issue of mandatory identification and identification tags for bodies was discussed. As a result, regardless of the detailed clauses, the principle itself, "The burial or cremation of the deceased must be preceded by a careful examination of their corpse," was unanimously adopted.[73]

Another point of contention was the issue of how to handle "identification tags" for verifying soldiers' identity. The differences in the positions of each country became clear over how much should be stipulated in international treaties. The Portuguese representative proposed a form of hanging a metal plate from the neck with a string, but the Japanese representative expressed doubt about whether there was a need to stipulate it in an international treaty, as the Japanese military was already practicing the use of identification tags.[74] The French representative also argued that there was no need to make the use of identification tags an international obligation. As a result of a vote called by the chairman on whether to stipulate in the treaty that all armies should carry identification tags, it was concluded that this should not be stipulated in the treaty.

Furthermore, a vote was also taken on whether to explicitly state the "obligation to send items that enable the identification of the deceased to the country to which the deceased belonged." On this point, the Russian representative introduced the fact that information exchange for creating lists of the wounded and sick was conducted during the Russo-Japanese War, and argued that it was practically possible.[75] As a result of the vote, it was unanimously decided to adopt this.

Thus, in the 1906 Geneva Convention, Article 3 stipulated the protection of the wounded and dead on the battlefield, as well as the inspection of bodies before burial, and Article 4 stipulated the sending of identification tags and lists of the wounded and sick to the other side. These provisions would later be further detailed in the 1949 Geneva Conventions.[76] In addition, the 1949 Convention also stipulated the obligation to record the burial sites of the war dead, which was not stipulated in the 1906 Convention.

---

[71] Ibid.

[72] Ibid., 71–73.

[73] Ibid., 76.

[74] Ibid.

[75] Ibid., 77.

[76] Articles 14, 15, and 16 of the First Geneva Convention of 1949.

The Ideological Foundation of the Protection of the War Dead

From the late nineteenth century to the early twentieth century, the norms for the protection of the war dead were gradually put into practice and eventually codified. Behind this was a network of international law scholars, among whom Gustave Moynier of the ICRC made a significant contribution. He served as president of the ICRC for about forty years from 1863, during which time he devoted his efforts to the establishment, maintenance, and revision of the Geneva Conventions.[77] Although not as well known as Henri Dunant, in terms of the process of codifying the norms for the protection of the war dead, it can be said that he played a more important role than Dunant, serving as chairman at international conferences on numerous occasions.

On what vision of an international order did Moynier base his discussion of international humanitarian law? His most important work in this regard is *Etude sur la Convention de Genève*, published in 1870.[78] This book, which coincided with the outbreak of the Franco-German War, did not receive sufficient recognition at the time, but it systematically discusses the international order that underpins international humanitarian law.

Moynier sees the development of international humanitarian law as part of the progress of civilization. As humanity progresses, it moves towards compliance with the law, and when it falls into barbarism, it moves towards armed conflict.[79] The nineteenth century in which he lived saw more protection of human life than previous centuries but, according to Moynier, the destination is still far ahead.[80] War, the symbol of human barbarism, is by no means gone, however, Moynier argues that public opinion has come to see war as a shame of humanity. Here lies the possibility of progress; as the power of public opinion grows, war should also gradually be restricted. He points out that with the development of means of information, events on the battlefield are becoming increasingly unable to escape the eyes of the world.[81]

Moynier states that even if war does not disappear, it is not at all in its former form.[82] That is, the methods of war are being restricted by international humanitarian law, and this is the development of civilization itself. Unfortunately, progress in military practice is slow, and old norms persist within the military. Therefore, what is needed today is to properly revise the legal rules concerning war.[83] It is necessary to codify what is allowed and what is prohibited; for example, wartime looting, infringement of private property rights, and massacres of prisoners of war and defenseless civilians should be prohibited. One of the results of such codification was the Geneva Convention of 1864, which needs to be spread through education so as for public

[77] François Bugnion, *Gustave Moynier: 1826–1910* (Geneva: Éditions Slatkine, 2010).

[78] Moynier, *Study on the Geneva Convention.*

[79] Ibid., 1.

[80] Ibid., 2–3.

[81] Ibid., 12.

[82] Ibid., 4.

[83] Ibid., 6.

opinion to develop.[84] Public opinion is "the best guardian" of international law, and compliance with the Geneva Convention depends on public opinion.[85]

Moynier thought that in the nineteenth century, the spirit of charity and humanity is spreading and beginning to have influence among mankind. This is happening through empathy for war victims and, indeed, the establishment of numerous aid societies around the world is evidence of this, he argued.[86] Also, he stated that this spirit of humanity is being embodied in some legal systems and practices, for example, the abolition of the right to confiscate inheritance and the right to plunder shipwrecks, as well as the protection of private property rights during international disputes.[87] The underlying premise was that war is between states, not between individuals. This was borrowed from the words of Jean Portalis, a French jurist of the eighteenth century. Even if countries are at war, the individuals who make up those countries no longer consider individuals as enemies. Since war belongs to the public domain, private rights such as property rights must be protected.[88]

Moynier was not the only one who had such an international law thought. The network of international law scholars called "the men of 1873" by Martti Koskenniemi had common ideological characteristics.[89] In Moynier's previous book, the works of Johann K. Bluntschli, Fyodor F. Martens, and Charles Vergé are quoted, and the influence from their international law thought is strongly reflected. They were cosmopolitans of liberalism, and many were politically moderate. What they focused on was not state sovereignty, but society. The legal consciousness of society was considered the source of law. The same was true for international law, where the legal consciousness inherent in a society composed of states made international law legal. The role of international law scholars is to articulate such unspoken legal consciousness, and to promote further development of society and law. As international humanitarian law is also international law, interpretation and codification by international law scholars is necessary, and "the men of 1873" actually worked on this codification.

Moynier and others actively created a network of international law scholars, published journals on international law, and advanced projects on the codification of international humanitarian law. One of the triggers was the Franco-German War. In this war, the Geneva Convention was not observed more than the Red Cross officials imagined. Codification by legal scholars was essential for the spread of international

---

[84] Ibid., 296–97.

[85] Ibid., 301.

[86] Ibid., 9.

[87] Ibid., 10.

[88] Ibid., 11–12.

[89] Martti Koskenniemi, *The Gentle Civilizer of Nations: The Rise and Fall of International Law 1870–1960* (Cambridge: Cambridge University Press, 2001), Ch. 1; Besty Baker Röben, "The Method behind Bluntschli's Modern International Law," *Journal of History of International Law*, no. 4 (2002); Dietrich Schindler, "J. C. Bluntschli's Contribution to the Law of War," in *Promoting Justice, Human Rights and Conflict Resolution through International Law*, ed. Marcelo G. Kohen (Leiden: Martinus Nijhoff Publishers, 2007).

law. Moynier approached Gustave Rolin-Jaequemyns, a Belgian jurist, and proposed creating a network of international law scholars.

Around the same time, Francis Lieber of the United States made a similar proposal to Rolin-Jaequemyns. Lieber was born in Berlin and served in the Prussian army during the Napoleonic Wars, but later immigrated to the United States and obtained a professorship in political economy at a university. When the Civil War began, he became a legal advisor to the Union Army and created General Order No. 100, which codified the customary laws regarding the methods of war in Europe.[90] This became known as the "Lieber Code" and had a significant influence on European international law scholars, including Bluntschli, as a representative example of the codification of international law.[91]

In September 1873, international law scholars from Europe and the United States, including Moynier, held their first meeting in Ghent, Belgium, and established the International Law Association. After the Russo-Turkish War, they published the Oxford Manual in 1880 to encourage legislation on war within each country. Again, the protection of the dead was stipulated in this manual (Articles 19 and 20). Thus, from the second half of the nineteenth century until the revision of the Geneva Convention in 1906, the network of international law scholars supported the work of codifying international humanitarian law.

It must be noted that there were "Others" who were rarely mentioned in the thoughts of these international law scholars. By viewing international law as something based on European civilization, regions outside of European civilization found it difficult to possess legal personality equal to that of the European powers.[92] The existence of Japan is a good example of these boundaries of civilization, who tried to enter the boundaries of civilization as defined by Western countries by adhering to (and promoting) international humanitarian law in the Sino-Japanese War and the Russo-Japanese War.

As mentioned earlier, norms such as benevolence and charity exist at the core of the civilization that underpins international humanitarian law. Nagao Ariga accurately understood this. While benevolism originates from Christianity, Japan is not a Christian country, a point which Ariga tried to theoretically overcome. According to Ariga, benevolism had already left Christianity and became a general culture. Also, Japan had benevolence based on Bushido, and could accept the benevolism of Western countries without any problem.[93] Being able to accept the benevolism unilaterally defined by the West was indeed meeting the standards of civilization.

---

[90] Silja Vöneky, "Francis Lieber (1798–1872)," in *The Oxford Handbook of the History of International Law*, ed. Bardo Fassbender and Anne Peters (Oxford: Oxford University Press, 2012).

[91] Schindler, "J. C. Bluntschli's Contribution to the Law of War.

[92] Koskenniemi, *The Gentle Civilizer of Nations*, Ch. 2.

[93] Nagao Ariga, *Bankoku Senshi Kōhō: Rikusen Jōkikku* (Rikugun Daigakkō, 1894), 53–55.

2.5 Management of Combat Deaths by States

Management of Combat Casualty Information

The protection of the war dead was indeed codified in the Geneva Convention of 1906, which was first put to the test in practice with the outbreak of World War I in 1914. The most significant characteristic of this war was the enormous number of war dead which, according to historian Antoine Prost's estimates, exceeded 10 million in total.[94] Therefore, it was by no means easy for governments and militaries of various countries to grasp the data of the war dead during the war. There were also issues such as how to track the rapidly increasing number of missing persons, how to handle the bodies that were piling up every day, and how to record the burial sites. In conclusion, each country, not to mention the enemy forces, struggled to deal with even their own military dead and were forced to drastically overhaul their systems.

According to Prost, the number of French war dead in World War I was approximately 1.4 million (including those from the colonies). Compared simply with the Franco-German War, about ten times as many French people died. At this time, the war dead were already respected for their individual identities, and there was a system in place to officially confirm whether they had died. In France, an administrative order of July 23, 1894, required the explicit indication of whether a soldier's death occurred during combat, and the health regulations of 1910 stipulated that the circumstances of the war dead should be recorded,[95] however, such laws ceased to function in the first month of World War I when a large number of war dead occurred. The task of collecting information on such a large number of war dead overwhelmed the administrative capacity of the military. As a result, by the end of 1915, the requirements for death declarations were relaxed by a new law.[96]

Even on the battlefield, the collection of death records for each soldier was extremely difficult. The military mainly managed the soldiers' records on the battlefield, but military hospitals and domestic sanitary units were under the jurisdiction of the city, with this difference in jurisdiction hindering the centralized management of information. Also, each military unit had a person in charge of managing the soldiers' records, who had to confirm each individual's death before creating a death certificate. However, as the fighting intensified, it became difficult for the record keepers to go to the scene and confirm the deaths, with the large number of casualties also hindering the investigation. In the end, paperwork on the ground was difficult, and it sometimes took several months for a single case.[97]

---

[94] Antoine Prost, "The Dead," in *The Cambridge History of The First World War*, ed. Jay Winter (Cambridge: Cambridge University Press, 2014).

[95] Emmanuel Penicaut, "Quand le militaire se fait officier d'état civil: l'état civil militaire pendant la Grande Guerre," in *Le soldat et la mort dans la Grande Guerre*, dir. Isabelle Homer and Emmanuel Pénicaut (Rennes, 2016), 81.

[96] Ibid., 82.

[97] Ibid., 84; Alexandre Lafon, "Un difficile bilan chiffré des pertes combattantes: l'exemple français," in *Le soldat et la mort dans la Grande Guerre*, dir. Isabelle Homer and Emmanuel Pénicaut (Rennes, 2016), 43.

In the spring of 1915, France introduced oval metal identification tags, aiming to make the identification of bodies more reliable. As the war progressed, France improved the design of the identification tags by adding a notch, making it possible to split them in two and leave one part with the body, that is, when a soldier died, someone from the same unit would take one part as evidence of death, and the other part would be left for identification when the body was collected after the battle.[98] This design of splitting the metal plate into two was also introduced in Germany around the same time. However, soldiers often lost or did not carry their identification tags.[99]

In France, the Administrative Documents Bureau was overwhelmed with processing vast amounts of information and was forced to adapt to the situation. Similarly, the Relief Bureau for bereaved families, the Pension and Gratitude Bureau for the injured, and the Inheritance Department for bereaved families also fell into the same situation. The state began to care not only for the death of soldiers but also for their families, however, due to the organizational structure, the functions were dispersed and weak, and the government had to integrate related tasks. Unsurprisingly, the number of staff had to be increased.[100]

Despite the vast number of deaths in the war, French citizens could not know the exact number of war dead during the war, because the military authorities avoided revealing accurate numbers for fear of causing anxiety among the people and informing the enemy of the situation. Not only France but also other warring nations tended to calculate each other's losses and present false numbers to their citizens.[101] The first time the total number of war dead was publicly revealed in France was in a parliamentary report in December 1918, after the end of the war: 1,385,000 as of November 1, 1918, of which 1,071,000 died and 314,000 were missing.[102]

As we have seen so far, France initially struggled to manage information about war dead during World War I, but by the end of the war, the state had significantly strengthened its ability to grasp and manage the number of war dead and to collect and convey information about individual deaths.

Tracking Missing Persons Through the Red Cross Network

As the number of deaths increased, so did the number of missing persons. The pain of the families of soldiers who went missing became a major issue during World War I, with the Red Cross network playing a crucial role in this. First, the International Committee of the Red Cross (ICRC), based in Geneva, established the International Prisoner of War Information Agency on August 21, 1914, just after the outbreak of war, which was to receive prisoner lists from the prisoner information bureaus of the warring nations. In parallel with this, the International Prisoner of

98 Harouel-Bureloup, "Identifier les corps des militaires morts au combat," 386.

99 Ashbridge and Verdegem, "Identity Discs," 4.

100 Penicaut, "Quand le militaire se fait officier d'état civil," 86–87.

101 Lafon, "Un difficile bilan chiffré des pertes combattantes," 45.

102 Ibid., 49.

War Information Agency collected information through its own investigations and responded to inquiries from the warring nations.[103]

National Red Cross societies also set up information bureaus in response to the ICRC's actions and tracked missing soldiers.[104] Families who sent off soldiers, when their loved ones went missing, contacted their respective national Red Cross societies. For example, the British Red Cross set up missing persons tracking offices not only in London but also in Paris and Boulogne, France, and responded to family inquiries.[105] The ICRC also worked to set up information bureaus in countries involved in the Eastern Front, such as Austria, Serbia, Russia, and Montenegro.[106]

Thus, a network of information bureaus in each warring nation, the ICRC's information agency, and the information bureaus of each national Red Cross society was established. The most important thing for this network to function was the exchange of information between each agency, but it was not that simple. For example, while there was immediate provision of prisoner information from Germany to France, provision from France did not progress as quickly, and there were times when the ICRC had to persuade France.[107]

Some Red Cross societies conducted interviews in hospitals outside of Europe to obtain information about missing persons. In World War I, battles were also fought in the Middle East and Africa, and associated military hospitals existed all over the world. Therefore, the British Red Cross also dispatched investigators to hospitals in places like Egypt,[108] but "[g]oing from bed to bed, searchers typically found only five useful patients for every hundred approached."[109] It was a task that required an enormous amount of effort.

In this war, not only was the protection of the war dead a concern, but violations of international humanitarian law were also rampant. As a result, the ICRC received numerous complaints of violations of humanitarian law from various national Red Cross societies. The ICRC, therefore, called for compliance with international humanitarian law and published cases that might involve violations of humanitarian law in the ICRC Bulletin. However, the ICRC only published the cases that were reported to it and avoided conducting its own investigations into them.[110]

---

[103] André Durand, *From Sarajevo to Hiroshima* (Geneva: Henry Dunant Institute, 1984), 35–40.

[104] Ibid., 40.

[105] Robert Sackville-West, *The Searchers: The Quest for the Lost of the First World War* (London: Bloomsbury, 2021), Ch. 1.

[106] Durand, *From Sarajevo to Hiroshima*, 41.

[107] Ibid., 41.

[108] Sackville-West, *The Searchers*, Ch. 2.

[109] Eric F. Schneider, "The British Red Cross Wounded and Missing Enquiry Bureau: A Case of Truth-Telling in the Great War," *War in History* 4, no. 3 (1997): 299.

[110] Lindsey Cameron, "The ICRC in the First World War: Unwavering Belief in the Power of Law?" *International Review of the Red Cross* 97, no. 900 (2015): 1099–120.

Management of Bodies and Burial Sites

When a large number of soldiers died, they had to be buried in some way. During World War I, many warring nations idealized the practice of burying each fallen soldier in a coffin and having the state clearly understand their name and burial location. Measures were taken to prevent soldiers from becoming unidentified bodies; for example, they were equipped with tags that clearly identified them, military personnel recorded the burial sites after confirming the dead, and items that could identify the fallen soldiers were left on the crosses erected at temporary burial sites.[111] However, on the battlefield, amidst intense fighting, there were many bodies left unburied, not only of enemy soldiers but also of a country's own troops, emitting a terrible stench. Also, for sanitary reasons, there were many cases where multiple bodies were buried in one grave; before 1915 in particular, soldiers who died on the front lines were often buried collectively. Even so, efforts were made to erect a cross for each soldier. In cases where burial had to be rushed for military reasons, bodies were sometimes buried in holes made by shells or in trenches.[112]

In early 1915, Britain established the Graves Registration Commission (later reorganized as the Imperial War Graves Commission) to centrally manage bodies and burial sites. The leader of this commission was Fabian Ware. At the start of the war, he worked as a Red Cross member, using cars to search for and transport wounded soldiers on the battlefield. During his activities, he came across the grave of a British casualty, with a makeshift cross erected there, but no one had recorded the location of the grave or the identity of the fallen soldier. Ware and other military and government officials strongly felt the need to record such temporary burial sites and established an organization for that purpose.[113] Thus, in Britain, the Red Cross complemented the functions of the state, and it was formally reorganized as an organization of the state.

Amid the massive number of war deaths, issues arose such as whether to eventually repatriate the bodies to their home countries or bury them where they fell in battle. In all warring nations, a considerable number of bereaved families wished to bury the bodies of fallen soldiers in their home countries. In Germany, the exhumation and repatriation of bodies by bereaved families was not prohibited, as it was considered a private matter. The United States made it a principle to repatriate the bodies of its soldiers. France and Belgium initially prohibited the personal exhumation of bodies, but soon allowed it. Only Britain prohibited the personal exhumation and repatriation of bodies, and thoroughly promoted local burial. The basis for this was egalitarianism, which held that all war dead should be treated equally, regardless of social or military rank.[114]

---

[111] Flucher, "Modes et lieux d'inhumation," 114.

[112] Ibid., 114–16.

[113] Sackville-West, *The Searchers*, 128–33.

[114] Dominiek Dendooven, ""Bringing the Dead Home": Repatriation, Illegal Repatriation and Expatriation of British Bodies during and after," in *Bodies in Conflict: Corporeality, Materiality and Transformation*, ed. Paul Cornish and Nicholas J. Saunders (London: Routledge, 2014).

However, while Britain advocated egalitarianism, it treated the burial of soldiers from the colonies differently. Especially in wars fought in Africa, many soldiers from India and Africa were mobilized, but their burial methods were distinguished from those of white soldiers. According to Michelle Barrett, who studied this issue, "the Africans who had fought and died as soldiers or lost their lives as porters, upwards of 200,000 of them, had not reached "the stage of civilisation" where they would appreciate individual graves and their remains were allowed to "revert to nature", unmarked."[115]

*

From the nineteenth to the early twentieth century, the protection of war dead became an international norm in Europe. Behind this was the issue of a large number of missing persons caused by various wars, including the Austro-Prussian War. At international conferences aimed at making the methods of war more humane, the pain of the families of the missing was addressed, and rules were established for the protection of bodies and the collection of information about the war dead. The ICRC supported this process of international standardization.

In World War I, practices based on these norms were attempted, but they were not always successful. The states could not keep up with the processing of the massive number of missing and dead soldiers. Nevertheless, a system gradually emerged for states to manage the deaths of their nationals (as soldiers). This international norm is still valid in the twenty-first century international community, and the ICRC is still playing the same role and function in the Ukraine War.

[115] Michèle Barrett, "Sent Missing in Africa," http://www.michelebarrett.com/wp-content/uploads/2019/11/Sent-Missing-in-Africa.pdf, 2. Also, Michèle Barrett, "White Graves and Natives," in *Bodies in Conflict: Corporeality, Materiality, and Transformation*, ed. Paul Cornish and Nicholas J. Saunders (London: Routledge, 2014); Michèle Barrett, "Subalterns at War: First World War Colonial Forces and the Politics of the Imperial War Graves Commission," *Interventions* 9, no. 3: 451–74. For a similar issue in France, see Sherman, *The Construction of Memory in Interwar France*, 101.

Chapter 3
Evolution of Civilian Protection Norms

Contents

Abstract This chapter examines the concept of civilians and the evolution of civilian protection norms. To this end, it analyzes the changing perception of civilians throughout the history of war. Prior to World War II, civilians were perceived as both vulnerable and as potential guerrillas resisting military occupation. However, during World War II, with the Nazi German occupation and large-scale bombing of urban areas, civilians were redefined as subjects that should be actively protected. Then, in 1949, the Fourth Geneva Convention was created, and civilian protection norms were codified. In it, civilians were categorized as entities to be protected, with conditions attached, in situations such as occupation, aerial bombing, and civil war.

The United Nations High Commissioner for Human Rights (OHCHR) has been regularly publishing the number of civilian casualties in the Ukraine War that began in February 2022. For example, data from August 22, 2022, indicated that 13,477 civilians were killed or injured, of which 5,587 died and 7,890 were injured.[1] Why go to the trouble of announcing the number of civilian casualties? This is because there is an international norm that belligerent countries should not target civilians in war. Specifically, this is stipulated in the Fourth Geneva Convention, concluded in 1949. As we saw in the previous chapter, the management of soldiers' deaths in Europe began in the late nineteenth century, but when and how did civilian deaths become an issue? This chapter provides an overview of the history of the development of civilian protection norms.

The 1949 Geneva Conventions have a very complicated structure. Among them, the civilian protection norms of the Fourth Convention are very difficult to understand. The reason is that civilians were a very ambivalent existence. Until that time,

[1] OHCHR, "Ukraine: Civilian Casualty Update 22 August 2022," August 22, 2022, https://www.ohchr.org/en/news/2022/08/ukraine-civilian-casualty-update-22-august-2022.

M. Igarashi, *War and Data on Armed Conflicts*, Evidence-Based Approaches to Peace and Conflict Studies 14, https://doi.org/10.1007/978-981-97-6418-1_3

civilians had been portrayed as participants in arbitrary and despotic wars, subject to the whims of monarchs, resulting in the loss of their private property and, in the worst-case scenario, their lives. In essence, they were portrayed as vulnerable and pitiable individuals. However, they were also depicted as potential military adversaries, either through conscription or uprising en masse against occupying forces. Alternatively, they were regarded as essential contributors to the war economy in the rear. In this case, civilians are a military threat. In other words, civilians have completely different characteristics depending on the situation; sometimes they were passive and peaceful, and sometimes they were combative and dangerous. In 1949, how did the international community depict this ambivalent existence of civilians in international humanitarian law, and how did it stipulate their protection? We should analyze its formulation.

3.1 Who Are Civilians?

From the Innocent to Civilians

Who are civilians is actually a difficult question. Generally, civilians are private citizens who do not belong to the military and are not participating in combat. However, strictly speaking under international law, this is not easily determined. There are many studies on civilian protection in war.[2] What kind of views are held in these previous studies?

There is a certain common view on the definition and scope of civilians. First, the opposite concept of civilians is combatants. As Robert Schütte wrote, "to define the "civilian", we have to define the "combatant" in the first place."[3] In fact, the definition and scope of civilians have been directly influenced by the fluctuations in the definition and scope of combatants. However, according to Helen M. Kinsella, known for her historical research on civilian protection, it was not until the nineteenth century that civilians in Europe became the antithesis of combatants.[4] Prior to that, in medieval Europe, there existed the concept of "immunity" that innocent humans

---

[2] The classical preceding studies are known to be Geoffrey Best, *Humanity in Warfare: The Modern History of the International Law of Armed Conflicts* (London: Weidenfeld and Nicolson, 1980), and Geoffrey Best, *War and Law since 1945* (Oxford: Clarendon Press, 1994). Hellen M. Kinsella was the first to tackle the issue of the history of the definition and scope of civilians in her work, *The Image before the Weapon: A Critical History of the Distinction between Combatant and Civilian* (Ithaca, N.Y.: Cornell University Press, 2011).

[3] Robert Schütte, *Civilian Protection in Armed Conflicts: Evolution, Challenges and Implementation* (Wiesbaden: Springer VS, 2015), 20. Similar points are made by Kinsella, *The Image before the Weapon*, 6–7.

[4] Kinsella, *The Image before the Weapon*, 28–29.

should be exempted from the targets of war.[5] In the modern era, this category of "innocent humans" has gradually been replaced by "civilians."[6]

Secondly, historically, there have been many people and areas that were considered outside the application of civilian protection norms. In particular, in the international community before decolonization, the European powers imposed a dichotomy of civilization/non-civilization, and in wars in non-civilized areas, the distinction between civilians and combatants was often deemed unnecessary.[7] They could kill everyone indiscriminately. In other words, the definition and scope of civilians were not only a pair with those of combatants, but there was also a category of "people in non-civilized areas" outside this dichotomy. The struggle over decolonization was not considered an armed conflict under international law for some time, even after the establishment of the Geneva Conventions.[8]

Thirdly, regarding the 1949 Geneva Conventions, which marked a watershed in the development of international humanitarian law,[9] the Fourth Geneva Convention was a groundbreaking one that directly stipulated civilians as protected subjects. Indeed, the 1907 Hague Land Warfare Convention also included provisions related to civilian protection. However, the word "civilians' is almost non-existent there; what is mainly referred to are "inhabitants," and it is only indirectly mentioned in the context of how combatants conduct combat. In the Fourth Convention, civilian protection is the main theme, and it is detailed. Who are the civilians in the 1949 Geneva Conventions? Even in this convention, civilians were not positively defined. However, there was certainly an image of civilians envisioned in the process of drafting and adopting the Fourth Geneva Convention.

---

[5] Richard Shelly Hartigan, *The Forgotten Victim: A History of the Civilian* (Chicago: Precedent, 1982); Colm McKeogh, *Innocent Civilians: The Morality of Killing in War* (Basingstoke: Palgrave, 2002).

[6] Hartigan, *The Forgotten Victim.*

[7] Frédéric Mégret, "From "Savages" to "Unlawful Combatants": A Postcolonial Look at International Law's "Other"", in *International Law and Its Others*, ed. Anne Orford (Cambridge: Cambridge University Press, 2006); Kinsella, *The Image before the Weapon.*

[8] Huw Bennett, *Fighting the Mau Mau: The British Army and Counter-Insurgency in the Kenya Emergency* (Cambridge: Cambridge University Press, 2013), 61–82; Fabian Klose, *Human Rights in the Shadow of Colonial Violence*, trans. Dona Geyer (Philadelphia: University of Pennsylvania Press, 2013), 92–137.

[9] Hisakazu Fujita, *International Humanitarian Law, Revised and Enlarged* (Tokyo: Yu-Shindo, 2003) [Japanese], 25–27; Giovanni Mantilla, "The Origins and Evolution of the 1949 Geneva Conventions and the 1977 Additional Protocols," in *Do the Geneva Conventions Matter?*, ed. Matthew Evangelista and Nina Tannenwald (New York: Oxford University Press, 2017), 45.

3.2 Image of Civilians Before World War II

Limitation to the Public Domain

How were civilians perceived before the establishment of the Geneva Conventions in 1949? To understand this, it is necessary to note that two opposing movements concerning civilians in war progressed in Europe from the eighteenth century onwards. One was the movement to limit war to the relationship between states (the public domain). According to this view, war was fundamentally an act of hostility between monarchs, and ordinary citizens were either distinguished from it or, at worst, only incidentally incorporated into the hostile relationship. The other was the movement to mobilize the entire nation for war. In the nineteenth century, with the development of nationalism, civilians were more likely to become soldiers through conscription or irregular soldiers attacking occupying forces. They also became the mainstay of the military economy, supporting the army's supplies from the home front.

According to military historian Michael Howard, "By the eighteenth-century European wars were being conducted by professional armed forces of a kind with which we would be familiar today."[10] As the system of maintaining and arming the military even in peacetime was established, the military developed its own subculture, i.e., its own customs and habits, and became a distinct entity from other social strata.[11] As the military and civilian society separated, a movement emerged to limit the targets of attack in war to soldiers. There are two representative theorists of this movement, the first being Emmerich de Vattel, a Swiss international law scholar active in the eighteenth century. In his *The Law of Nations* (1758), he divides the concept of "enemy" into "private enemy" and "public enemy."[12] The former is an entity that seeks to harm "us" out of personal motives, while the latter is an entity that uses military force against "us" for the restoration of rights or political claims.

According to Vattel, war is an act in which the citizens of the parties become "public enemies" of each other. When a sovereign declares war on another sovereign, their respective citizens also become "public enemies." However, for those who find it difficult to participate in combat, such as women and children, they must be distinguished from the enemy.[13] If the military wins the battle, it will occupy the opponent's territory, and in the occupied area, the military can acquire (plunder) public property. However, the private property of individual citizens is, in principle, protected.[14]

---

[10] Michael Howard, *War in European History* (Oxford: Oxford University Press, 2009), 54.

[11] Ibid.

[12] Emer de Vattel, *The Law of Nations, Or, Principles of the Law of Nature, Applied to the Conduct and Affairs of Nations and Sovereigns, with Three Early Essays on the Origin and Nature of Natural Law and on Luxury*, ed. and with an Introduction by Béla Kapossy and Richard Whitmore (Indianapolis: Liberty Fund, 2008), Book III, Ch. V, para. 69.

[13] Ibid., Book III, Ch. V, para. 72.

[14] Ibid., Book III, Ch. XIII, para. 193–200.

More radical than Vattel was Jean-Jacques Rousseau. In his *The Social Contract* (1762), he argued, "War then is a relation, not between man and man, but between State and State, and individuals are enemies only accidentally, not as men, nor even as citizens."[15] According to this position, civilians not participating in combat are not parties to the war and are naturally excluded from attack. This argument was not limited to Rousseau; Jean Portalis, a French jurist of the seventeenth century, also argued to limit war to the relationship between states, that is, to the public domain.[16] This thesis was later called the Rousseau-Portalis Principle.[17]

At the beginning of the nineteenth century, as seen in Chap.2, progress in the establishment of international legal principles regarding warfare was well underway, but its main theme was always the treatment of soldiers, and civilians were almost left out, except for those engaged in humanitarian activities. That does not mean that civilians were not involved in wars from the eighteenth to the nineteenth centuries; in the eighteenth century, European armies mainly obtained food for soldiers and horses locally,[18] which could be through trade or plunder. For example, Napoleon emphasized local conscription in order to move his troops quickly and widely during wars.[19] Also, in scorched earth tactics, villages located on the enemy's route were burned to hinder the enemy's supply. Such methods of supply continued even in the second half of the nineteenth century, when railways were used in wars, bringing revolutionary changes to the movement of personnel and goods.[20] Even though civilians continued their daily lives, they were involved in the war through conscription.

The Era of National Mobilization

In late eighteenth-century Europe, there was also a movement for all citizens to become the subject of war. After the French Revolution, the revolutionary government was forced to reorganize the army to counter threats from foreign countries such as Austria and Prussia. As a result, an army was established that mixed the old army that remained after the revolution and the newly mobilized citizenry.[21] The French army expanded significantly through reorganization, but the quality of the soldiers declined and local conscription led to many civilians becoming involved and

[15] Jean Jacques Rousseau, *The Social Contract or Principles of Political Right*, trans. G.D.H. Cole (London and Toronto: J.M. Dent and Sons, 1923), Ch. 4.

[16] Eyal Benvenisti, "The Origins of the Concept of Belligerent Occupation," *Law and History Review* 26, no. 3 (2008): 625–26.

[17] Best, *Humanity in Warfare*, 96–97.

[18] Martin Van Creveld, *Supplying War: Logistics from Wallenstein to Patton* (Cambridge: Cambridge University Press, 2004), 26–39.

[19] Ibid., 40–70.

[20] Ibid., 97–103.

[21] Lars Mjøset and Stephen Van Holde, "Killing for the State, Dying for the Nation: An Introductory Essay on the Life Cycle of Conscription into Europe's Armed Forces," in *The Comparative Study of Conscription in the Armed Forces*, Vol. 20 (2002), 33; Howard, *War in European History*, Ch. 5.

subsequently victims.[22] Prussia also began to mobilize its citizens against the French army through conscription.[23]

By the late nineteenth century, conscription of citizens became institutionalized in continental Europe.[24] Concurrently, as nationalism proliferated and matured across diverse regions, wars assumed the character of "clashes between nations." In the early nineteenth century, even Napoleon's army was said to be half foreign, but by the late nineteenth century, most of the members of the army were soldiers from their own country.[25]

When the entire nation began to be mobilized for war as soldiers, civilians became a potential military threat. At this time, civilians became an issue in war, especially in the case of occupation. In such situations, the attacking side would station troops within enemy territory. At that time, the entire nation could take up arms and resist, posing a significant threat to the attackers. Prussian military officer Carl Von Clausewitz referred to such battles as "general uprisings" in his *On War* (1832–34), explaining their characteristics as "the element of resistance will exist everywhere and nowhere."[26] This is, in a sense, guerrilla warfare or irregular warfare. He pointed out that especially in areas where the transportation network is undeveloped and villages are scattered, it was difficult to punish residents through looting and burning, making it difficult to respond to resistance movements.[27] In fact, during the Franco-German War of 1870–71, Prussian army was tormented by guerrilla warfare by French citizens and took retaliatory measures.[28] Hence, during the nineteenth century, resistance and retaliatory actions in occupied territories were commonly undertaken.[29]

The perception that the people of occupied territories are a threat can be inferred from the 1907 Hague Convention on Land Warfare. In its first and second articles, it clearly states the requirements for combatants, and if the people of a region (not an occupied territory) that has been invaded rise up and fulfill obligations such as openly carrying weapons, the uprising people are granted the right to be treated as prisoners of war. However, in areas occupied by the enemy, the uprising of the people was not considered a legitimate means of resistance. Instead, in occupied territories,

[22] Karma Nabulsi, *Traditions of War: Occupation, Resistance, and the Law* (Oxford: Oxford University Press, 1999), 22–27. For a specific example of the harm civilians suffered due to conscription by the French army at the time, see Doina Pasca Harsanyi, "Surviving Napoleon. A Case Study of Small Town Discursive Strategies during the Piacentino Rebellion (1805–1806)," *Modern Italy* 22, no. 3 (June 2017).

[23] Mjøset and Van Holde, "Killing for the State," 35, 42.

[24] Ibid., 46–59.

[25] Ibid., 37.

[26] Carl Von Clausewitz, *On War*, ed. and trans. Michael Howard and Peter Paret (Princeton: Princeton University Press, 1976), 480.

[27] Ibid.

[28] Isabel V. Hull, *Absolute Destruction: Military Culture and the Practices of War in Imperial Germany* (Ithaca: Cornell University Press, 2005), 117–19.

[29] Nabulsi, *Traditions of War*, 19–65.

looting by the occupying forces was prohibited,[30] that is, the protection of private property rights was explicitly stated.

The Era of Total War

Civilians became a military threat not only in guerrilla warfare in occupied territories, but also as the main body of production activities at home. At the end of the nineteenth century, the arms industry grew massively and took on a public character,[31] and in World War I, the entire production activities of the state were tied to the execution of the war,[32] that is, the state began to mobilize all personnel and materials within its territory for war, marking the start of "total war." In total war, civilians also played an important role in the wartime economy.

Aerial bombing greatly changed the position of civilians. The new tactic of aerial bombing, which European countries began in Asia and Africa in the early twentieth century,[33] was also implemented in Europe during World War I. By World War II, it began to target urban areas in earnest. Initially, the targets of bombing were mainly factories directly involved in the war, such as weapons manufacturing, which served as the basis for justification. Subsequently, the targets of attack gradually expanded to include civilian residences.[34] The invention of incendiary bombs made the destruction of houses more efficient.[35] Moreover, the invention of nuclear weapons made the distinction between combatants and non-combatants meaningless. A representative example of aerial bombing during World War II is the 1945 Dresden bombing by the United Kingdom, which aimed to completely destroy the entire city, causing a strong dilemma between military necessity and moral demand for the implementers.[36] It was not much of an issue in the Asia-Africa region, but as soon as Europe became a battlefield, the mass killing of defenseless civilians became a major moral issue.[37]

In the United Kingdom, the bombing of Dresden was justified by the view that the bombing would demoralize the enemy's citizens and lead to surrender.[38] In other words, the will of the people was considered important in the decision to continue the war. Large-scale air raids involving civilians were also carried out in Tokyo.

---

[30] Hague Regulations of 1907, Annex to the Convention: Regulations Respecting the Laws and Customs of War on Land, Article 47; Amanda Alexander, "The Genesis of the Civilian," *Leiden Journal of International Law* 20 (2007): 364–65.

[31] William McNeil, *The Pursuit of Power* (Chicago: University of Chicago Press, 1982), 292.

[32] Ibid., 317–45.

[33] Sven Lindqvist, *A History of Bombing*, trans. Linda Haverty Rugg (London: Granta, 2012), Sect. 76–82.

[34] M. Kirby and R. Capey, "The Area Bombing of Germany in World War II: An Operational Research Perspective," *Journal of the Operational Research Society* 48, no. 7 (1997).

[35] Robert M. Neer, *Napalm: An American Biography* (Cambridge: The Belknap Press of Harvard University Press, 2013).

[36] M. Walzer, *Just and Unjust Wars: Moral Argument with Historical Illustrations* (S.l.: Allen Lane, 1977), 255–63; Tetsuo Maeda, *Thoughts on Strategic Bombing: Guernica, Chongqing, Hiroshima, Revised Edition* (Tokyo: Gaifūsha, 2006) [Japanese], 475–77.

[37] Mégret, "From "Savages" to "Unlawful Combatants.""

[38] Kirby and Capey, "The Area Bombing of Germany."

Moreover, atomic bombs were dropped on Hiroshima and Nagasaki, causing enormous damage. After the atomic bomb was dropped, the United States feared that its inhumanity would become known to the world and concealed information about the victims in its occupation policy.[39]

3.3 Establishment of the Geneva Conventions of 1949

Rapid developments after World War II

By 1949, civilians were seen as passive and peaceful, but also as the mainstay of war, and if faced with occupation, they could even be aggressive. In actual wars, they became targets of retaliation and attack. In 1947, Max Huber, the former president of the ICRC, said in a speech at a specialist meeting about the issue of civilian protection:

> [C]ivilians individually and the civilian population as a whole are not, as it were, protected under the Conventions. There are, it is true, provisions in the Hague Convention (IV) on War on Land that aim to protect the population of an occupied territory. They were not, however, sufficient to prevent–in 1914–18–deplorable acts in the absence of more precise limitations on the powers of the occupying power; in any event, these provisions apply only to occupied territories and do not cover civilians in enemy countries. They do not take into account new methods of warfare: the technical, political and economic methods of what is referred to as "total war".[40]

Many European countries experienced occupation by Nazi Germany and felt keenly the importance of protecting civilians (or, conversely, restraining the power of the occupying forces). There were also numerous cases of civilians in enemy countries being persecuted. In addition, as in Spain in the 1930s, many civilians lost their lives in civil wars. Above all, countless lives were lost due to large-scale air raids, including the dropping of nuclear weapons. Against this backdrop, the Fourth Geneva Convention was established at the international conference in 1949.

The path to the ratification of the treaty was fraught with extreme difficulty. The ICRC had attempted several times to codify civilian protection in the international community after the end of World War I, but all attempts had ended in failure.[41] However, things rapidly developed after World War II. The Nuremberg International Military Tribunal, which began immediately after the war, judged killings and abuses

---

[39] Masae Shiina, *Atomic Bomb Crime: Why Were the Survivors Abandoned?* (Tokyo: Otsuki Shoten, 1985) [Japanese].

[40] Cited in Catherine Rey-Schyrr, *From Yalta to Dien Bien Phu: History of the International Committee of the Red Cross 1945 to 1955* (Geneva: ICRC, 2017), 219. For the conservative nature of Huber's thoughts and actions, see Jean-Claude Favez, *The Red Cross and the Holocaust*, ed. and trans. John and Beryl Fletcher) (New York: Cambridge University Press, 1999), 129–30.

[41] Rey-Schyrr, *From Yalta to Dien Bien Phu*, 210–11.

against civilians during the war as crimes based on the International Military Tribunal Charter agreed upon by the victorious nations.[42]

In parallel with this, around the end of World War II, the ICRC, together with the Red Cross societies of various countries, once again began preparations for the revision of the Geneva Conventions, including the codification of civilian protection norms. The ICRC also sent memorandums regarding the revision of the Geneva Conventions to the victorious nations such as the United States, France, the United Kingdom, China, and the Soviet Union, urging them to send representatives to the expert meetings.[43]France and the United States agreed with this movement and immediately began preparations, but the United Kingdom showed a passive attitude. France, having experienced occupation by Nazi Germany, keenly felt the importance of civilian protection, while the United Kingdom feared that the provisions for civilian protection might create troublesome restrictions in future wars.[44] The most troubling for the ICRC was the Soviet Union, who had a distrust of the ICRC and replied that they would decline the invitation to the expert meeting.

In the spring of 1947, a year later than planned, the expert meeting was held. Approximately 80 experts from 15 countries gathered in Geneva, the venue, and exchanged views on the treaty based on the ICRC's draft.[45] In August of the following year, the seventeenth International Red Cross Conference was held in Stockholm, Sweden, with representatives from 56 countries participating. The Soviet Union officially declined to participate again, but sent an unofficial representative to gather information.[46] At this conference, the draft of the conventions was seriously considered, and a basis for the next diplomatic conference was created.[47] Finally, in April 1949, a diplomatic conference on the conclusion of international treaties for the protection of war victims was held in Geneva. Representatives from 64 countries, including the Soviet Union, participated.[48]

Civilians Protected by the Geneva Conventions

At the 1949 Geneva Conference, the existing three Geneva Conventions were revised, and a new Geneva Convention was established to regulate the protection of civilians. Before examining the contents of this new treaty, it needs to be briefly explained that the 1949 Geneva Conventions are a collective term for four treaties designed to protect victims of war. As we saw in the previous chapter, the history of the conventions began with the Geneva Convention for the Amelioration of the Condition of the

---

42 Principles of International Law Recognized in the Charter of the Nürnberg Tribunal and in the Judgment of the Tribunal, Principle VI (b) and (c).

43 Rey-Schyrr, *From Yalta to Dien Bien Phu*, 212–16.

44 Giovanni Mantilla, *Lawmaking under Pressure: International Humanitarian Law and Internal Armed Conflict* (Ithaca: Cornell University Press, 2020), 69–72.

45 Rey-Schyrr, *From Yalta to Dien Bien Phu*, 218.

46 Boyd von Dijk, ""The Great Humanitarian": The Soviet Union, the International Committee of the Red Cross, and the Geneva Conventions of 1949," *Law and History Review* 37, no. 1 (February 2019): 220–21.

47 Rey-Schyrr, *From Yalta to Dien Bien Phu*, 224–25.

48 For the motives of the Soviet Union's participation, see Dijk, "The Great Humanitarian.".

Wounded and Sick in Armed Forces in the Field (First Convention) established in 1864. Initially, only twelve countries signed, but it later expanded. In 1899, the Geneva Convention for the Amelioration of the Condition of Wounded, Sick and Shipwrecked Members of Armed Forces at Sea (Second Convention) was established, and in 1929, the Geneva Convention relative to the Treatment of Prisoners of War (Third Convention) was established. These three conventions were all about treating wounded, sick, and prisoners of war humanely. In other words, civilians were not directly protected.

At the 1949 Geneva Conference, the first to third conventions were revised. The provisions for the protection of the dead, seen in the previous chapter, became more detailed in this revision. More importantly, the Geneva Convention relative to the Protection of Civilian Persons in Time of War (the Fourth Geneva Convention) was newly created. Considering that until then only military personnel were protected, the establishment of the Fourth Geneva Convention was revolutionary. At the time, Paul Ruegger, the chairman of the ICRC, called the establishment of the Fourth Convention a "miracle"[49]; it was something that could limit a part of the sovereign acts of a state in war.

How were "civilians" defined in the Geneva Conventions? As mentioned at the beginning of this chapter, the conventions do not explicitly define civilians. Instead, they present several categories of civilians who are protected, that is, categories of who is protected under what circumstances and with what qualifications.[50] The specific categories of protected civilians can be summarized as follows (Table 3.1).

Thus, the Fourth Convention does not define civilians per se, but divides civilians into several categories and stipulates their protection. These categories were formed based on specific situations such as occupation, aerial bombing, and civil war.

---

[49] Rey-Schyrr, *From Yalta to Dien Bien Phu*, 252.

[50] Here, in order to interpret the status of civilians in Article 4, I referred to the conference records leading up to the conventions, ICRC's commentary, and especially the commentary on the Fourth Geneva Convention published in 1958 (Jean Pictet, ed., *Commentary IV Geneva Convention: Relative to the Protection of Civilian Persons in Time of War* (Geneva: International Committee of the Red Cross, 1958)). What is the ICRC's commentary? Generally, laws can have annotations. Laws can be abstract and have unclear wording, so annotations supplement their content. A commentary is not the law itself, but a document that presents the background and specific legal interpretation of the law. As it presents background and interpretation, a commentary has considerable influence. It cannot be ignored when considering the applicability of the law. The ICRC is an organization that has promoted the establishment of international humanitarian law, including the Geneva Conventions. Therefore, it is recognized as an authority in discussing legal interpretations of humanitarian law, and its commentary has a certain influence. The main focus here is the ICRC's commentary written in 1958, which was supervised by legal scholar Jean Pictet. During the diplomatic conference in 1949 when the Geneva Conventions were established, Pictet played an active role as the ICRC representative and head of the legal department. He was involved in drafting the 1949 conventions and was later called "the chief architect" of the conventions. For this point, see Rey-Schyrr, *From Yalta to Dien Bien Phu*, 214, note 15 and Alexandre Hay et al., "A Tribute to Jean Pictet," *International Review of the Red Cross* 19, no. 210 (June 1979): 115–29.

Table 3.1 Categories of civilians protected by the 1949 Geneva Conventions

Categories	Concrete image of civilians	Requirements to become a civilian	Main relevant articles
(A) Civilians under enemy control, such as during occupation	1. Inhabitants of occupied territory 2. Individuals with nationality of an enemy country residing in the territory of a conflicting party	Nationality	Fourth Geneva convention, Article 4
(B) Civilians exposed to attacks targeting the entire population, such as airstrikes	Wounded, sick, and aged persons, children under fifteen, expectant mothers and mothers of children under seven	Physical condition, age, gender	Fourth Geneva convention, Article 13–26
(C) Civilians in a state of civil war	People who do not directly engage in hostile activities	Activities	Common article 3

For Civilians to Gain Protection

Several questions arise from here. The Fourth Convention stipulates the protection of civilians, however, if a belligerent country violates this provision during combat and attacks and massacres civilians, who will prove that the person attacked was a civilian? Who will prove that their death cannot be justified by military necessity? Where should such claims be made? This book will scrutinize these issues in subsequent chapters, however, for the present, we should focus on the provisions outlined in the 1949 Geneva Conventions.

What about in the case of occupation? According to the treaty, civilians should be protected during occupation. But what if the occupying forces start to act brutally? As already mentioned, the Hague Land Warfare Convention did not recognize participation in resistance movements in occupied areas as a right of the residents. However, during World War II, guerrilla warfare against occupying forces was carried out in places like France under German occupation, and the interpretation of resistance movements by the people changed after the war. As a result, "members of organized resistance movements" were included in the scope of those protected under the first treaty of the 1949 Geneva Conventions (Article 13). In this way, when civilians join an organized resistance movement, they are classified as combatants and receive certain protection. In other words, civilians had the option of joining a resistance organization and acting as combatants (ceasing to be civilians) if they could not obtain protection under occupation. Indeed, the transition to combatant status did not guarantee humane treatment from occupying forces, rendering it an ineffective means for civilians to preserve their identity and secure protection.

What about in the case of air raids? During the 1949 Diplomatic Conference, the ICRC explored a proposal to obligate the parties to the conflict to establish safe zones to protect civilians from attacks such as air raids. Although the obligation was postponed due to military opposition from countries like the United Kingdom, provisions regarding the establishment of safe zones were included[51] (Article 15 of the Fourth Convention). If the parties to the conflict agree to establish a safe zone and it is realized, civilians may be able to receive protection by moving to the safe zone. The problem was how feasible it was to establish such a zone under armed conflict, and to what extent its safety could be ensured. In recent years, proposals have been made to establish safe zones and humanitarian corridors in conflicts such as the Syrian and Ukrainian wars to protect civilians from attacks and secure routes for them to move to safe places, but these have rarely been realized. For example, in Mariupol, attempts to establish humanitarian corridors were made several times, but tens of thousands of civilian lives were lost before it was realized.

Could someone other than the belligerents enforce the Fourth Geneva Convention? Who monitored the implementation of the Convention? In this regard, the Fourth Geneva Convention introduced a system called Protecting Powers. What are Protecting Powers? For example, in the case of war, there may be instances where citizens of one's own country are treated unfairly by the enemy country. In such cases, the interests of one's own citizens, who are under the power of the enemy country, are protected by another country. This is the system of Protecting Powers. This system was originally a system to monitor the treatment of prisoners of war and was codified in the nineteenth century,[52] and was expanded to the protection of civilians in the Geneva Conventions of 1949. However, the agreement of the warring parties is necessary to establish a Protecting Power. After World War II, the Falklands conflict in 1982 can be cited as a war where a Protecting Power was actually established, but such cases are not necessarily numerous.

Absence of Monitoring Actors

The Geneva Conventions of 1949 recognize the humanitarian activities of international NGOs such as the ICRC in the protection of civilians. Would it not be sufficient if they monitored the implementation of civilian protection? As we will see in the next chapter, the ICRC has warned the parties involved about violations of humanitarian law, but it has rarely, as a rule, appeal to public opinion. Furthermore, international judicial systems related to humanitarian law were proposed during the negotiation process from 1946, but they did not materialize due to opposition from the United Kingdom and the United States. The ICRC was also negative about the establishment of such international systems.[53] It was much later that international NGOs and the United Nations began to monitor the implementation of civilian protection (discussed

---

[51] *Final Record of the Diplomatic Conference of Geneva of 1949* (Berne: Federal Political Department, 1963), Vol. 2, Section A, 626–30; Best, *War and Law since 1945*, 116.

[52] Howard S. Levie, "Prisoners of War and the Protecting Power," *The American Journal of International Law* 55, no. 2 (April 1961).

[53] Mark Lewis, *The Birth of the New Justice: the Internationalization of Crime and Punishment, 1919–1950* (Oxford: Oxford University Press, 2014), 229–73; Boyd van Dijk, *Preparing for War: The Making of the Geneva Conventions* (Oxford: Oxford University Press, 2022), 265–95.

in Chap. 4). In the end, under the system of the Geneva Conventions of 1949, there were no actors to monitor the protection of civilians.

In the Korean War, which began in 1950 immediately after the establishment of the Geneva Conventions, a large number of civilians lost their lives. The Korean War was a war that began between the Democratic People's Republic of Korea (North Korea) and the Republic of Korea (South Korea), with the UN forces, mainly the US forces, siding with South Korea and China siding with North Korea. Although the Geneva Conventions had not yet come into effect in this war, the US Department of State conveyed its intention to respect the humanitarian norms of the Geneva Conventions to the ICRC.[54] Also, during the war, high-ranking officials of the US government and military repeatedly claimed that the US military was adhering to the norms of civilian protection. For example, US Secretary of State D. Acheson, during the war, in response to criticism that "UN forces are bombing and killing defenseless civilians," stated that UN air strikes in Korea had been "directly solely at military targets of the invader" and that these targets were "enemy troop concentrations, supply dumps, war plants, and communication lines."[55] However, the American military fired at the large number of refugees that had emerged, causing the No Gun Ri massacre (July 1950),[56] and launched a scorched earth campaign with large-scale air raids on various cities.[57] When a belligerent nation massacred civilians, no one in the world could record or report it, let alone punish it. This was the reality of civilian protection in the 1950s.

So, how does the Geneva Conventions regulate the case of civilian deaths? This is stipulated in Articles 129 to 131 of the Fourth Convention. These articles have in mind not air raids, but civilians detained by the enemy. According to this, when a detained civilian dies, a doctor must confirm it and create a death certificate stating the condition and cause of death, which must then be sent to the Protecting Power or the information bureau. The body must be buried individually, the location of the grave recorded, and this information notified to the country to which the deceased belonged. Furthermore, if the cause of death of a detained civilian is possibly due to crimes such as violence by the detaining side, the detaining country is obliged to take measures to investigate and prosecute. Certainly, such provisions have not always been effectively implemented in practice during actual wars.

*

[54] Sahr Conway-Lanz, "The Struggle to Fight a Humane War: The United States, the Korean War, and the 1949 Geneva Conventions," in *Do the Geneva Conventions Matter?*, ed. Matthew Evangelista and Nina Tannenwald (New York: Oxford University Press, 2017), 73.

[55] Secretary Acheson, "North Korea Slanders U.N. Forces to Hide Guilt of Aggression," *U.S. Department of State Bulletin*, September 18, 1950, 454.

[56] Charles J. Hanley, Sang-Hun Choe, and Martha Mendoza, *The Bridge at No Gun Ri: A Hidden Nightmare from the Korean War* (New York: Henry Holt and Co, 2001).

[57] Sahr Conway-Lanz, "The Ethics of Bombing Civilians After World War II: The Persistence of Norms Against Targeting Civilians in the Korean War," *The Asia–Pacific Journal* 12, no. 1 (2014).

In the 1949 Geneva Conventions, the protection of civilians was stipulated in the newly established Fourth Convention. Civilians were a dangerous existence that could take up arms and resist when their country was occupied. In the nineteenth century, civilians were a threat in this regard. However, during World War II, European countries experienced occupation by Nazi Germany and keenly felt the need to curb the power of the occupying country. There were many cases where their own citizens living in enemy countries were exposed to violence. Also, in this war, full-scale air raids on urban areas were carried out, and civilians were unilaterally massacred. Against this backdrop of changing circumstances, norms for civilian protection were codified in 1949.

This chapter started with the question of who is a civilian. In the Fourth Geneva Convention of 1949, civilians themselves were not defined, with instead several categories of protected civilians explicitly stated, that is, categories of who was protected under what circumstances and with what requirements. This Fourth Geneva Convention was a miraculous achievement, but an international system to implement it in reality was not yet established, because there were no actors to record and denounce any violations of the Geneva Conventions and to fight against the states. Sovereign states were too powerful in wars. In the next chapter, we will examine the historical process through which such actors, who record and denounce, emerged in the international community.

Chapter 4
Emergence of Conflict Witnesses

Contents

The international community, through the experience of World War II, finally codified the protection of civilians during wartime. However, the question of who would monitor its implementation remained. What is the situation in the world of the 2020s? In the Ukraine War that began in 2022, the Office of the United Nations High Commissioner for Human Rights (OHCHR) regularly investigates and publishes data on civilian casualties. Also, international NGOs such as Human Rights Watch denounce war crimes committed by the Russian military. Thus, now, UN human rights organizations and international NGOs often cooperate to monitor the implementation of international humanitarian law, such as the 1949 Geneva Conventions. The DAC generated by these humanitarian networks greatly influences the perception of people who are not directly involved in the war. When and how did UN human rights organizations and international NGOs start investigating and publishing human rights abuses and violations of humanitarian law in armed conflicts? This chapter traces the history of the emergence of such conflict witnesses.[1]

[1] As a preliminary study related to the monitoring of the implementation of international humanitarian law, there are Michael Barnett, *Empire of Humanity: A History of Humanitarianism* (Ithaca and London: Cornell University Press, 2011); Heike Krieger, ed., *Inducing Compliance with International Humanitarian Law: Lessons from the African Great Lakes Region* (Cambridge: Cambridge University Press, 2015); Philip Alston and Sarah Knuckey, eds., *The Transformation of Human Rights Fact-Finding* (New York: Oxford University Press, 2016); Mark Lattimer and Philippe Sands, eds., *The Gray Zone: Civilian Protection between Human Rights and the Laws of War* (Oxford: Hart Publishing, 2018).

M. Igarashi, *War and Data on Armed Conflicts*, Evidence-Based Approaches to Peace and Conflict Studies 14, https://doi.org/10.1007/978-981-97-6418-1_4

4.1 Silence of the International Committee of the Red Cross

The Silence of the International Committee of the Red Cross

The International Committee of the Red Cross (ICRC), a pioneer of international NGOs, emerged in the late nineteenth century and supported the development of international humanitarian law, as we saw in Chap. 2. However, both the ICRC and the national Red Cross societies were merely complementary to the activities of the state's military (especially medical activities and information gathering activities for missing persons). They were, so to speak, in an internationally recognized neutral political space and rarely confronted sovereign states directly. This led to an attitude of avoiding publicly criticizing the activities of sovereign states and testifying to their realities.[2]

The ICRC maintained this stance even during World War II, a time of countless humanitarian tragedies. For instance, the ICRC did not expose to the world the reality of the mass extermination of Jews by Nazi Germany (a point which has been criticized several times since the 1980s).[3] The ICRC's main activities during World War II were humanitarian aid activities requested by the Allies,[4] which special consideration had to be given to the political neutrality of the Swiss government, which had a significant influence on the ICRC's activities.[5] This was not only about the Holocaust; the ICRC also maintained silence on humanitarian crises such as the genocide of the Herero and Nama by Germany in Southwest Africa in the early twentieth century, and the use of poison gas by Italy in Ethiopia.[6]

What changed significantly after World War II, as seen in the previous chapter, was the codification of civilian protection norms by international law. In the 1930s, the ICRC attempted to codify civilian protection twice, but failed, only finally achieving this in the Geneva Conventions of 1949.[7] Also, the year before, the United Nations General Assembly adopted the Convention on the Prevention and Punishment of the Crime of Genocide (commonly known as the Genocide Convention), which made genocide, an act committed with intent to destroy, in whole or in part, a national, ethnic, racial, or religious group, a crime under international law. The concept of "genocide" in this sense was brought into this world by Raphael Lemkin, a Polish Jew, who survived two world wars and dedicated his life to campaigning for the

---

[2] David P. Forsythe, *The Humanitarians: The International Committee of the Red Cross* (Cambridge: Cambridge University Press, 2005), 194.

[3] As a representative study on this issue, Jean-Claude Favez, *The Red Cross and the Holocaust*, ed. and trans. John and Beryl Fletcher (New York: Cambridge University Press, 1999).

[4] Sebastien Farre, "The ICRC and the Detainees in Nazi Concentration Camps (1942–1945)," *International Review of the Red Cross* 94, no. 888 (Winter 2012).

[5] Ibid., 1403, 1408.

[6] I. Herrmann and D. Palmieri, "Humanitarianism and Massacres: The Example of the International Committee of the Red Cross," in *Resisting Genocide*, ed. J. Semelin, C. Andrieu, and S. Gensburger (Oxford: OUP, 2013); Forsythe, *Humanitarians*, 39.

[7] Forsythe, *Humanitarians*, 54–55.

punishment of mass extermination of minorities by states under international law.[8] The Genocide Convention might not exist without Lemkin's efforts. In the case of genocide, the distinction between civilians/soldiers is not directly related, but in terms of protecting humans from extermination, it is ideologically close to the Fourth Geneva Convention of 1949. While the Fourth Geneva Convention addresses civilian casualties related to war, the Genocide Convention addresses massacres regardless of whether it is peacetime or wartime. As mentioned in Chaps. 5 and 6, genocide was one of the major issues in the International Criminal Tribunal for the former Yugoslavia.

Biafra War

The Biafra War, which occurred in Nigeria from 1967 to 1970, was the first instance of NGOs conflicting with the sovereign state over war data. The causes of the Biafra War are still controversial, but the backdrop was regional and ethnic conflicts that intensified after decolonization. Shortly after decolonization, Nigeria was broadly divided into the north, centered on the Hausa-Fulani, the west, centered on the Yoruba, and the east, centered on the Igbo (although there were countless other ethnic groups). In July 1966, a coup was staged by Yakubu Gowon and others from the north, who opposed the centralized rule of Johnson Aguiyi-Ironsi, a general of Igbo descent. Although Gowon's coup was successful, only the eastern region, where the Igbo were the majority, continued to be governed by Chukwuemeka Ojukwu, who was appointed by General Ironsi. Also, as a result of this coup, persecution and massacres of people of Igbo descent increased in the north, resulting in refugees. When Gowon, who became the head of state, announced a reform of the state system, in May 1967, the east, led by Ojukwu, declared independence, and armed conflict broke out between the federal government and eastern Biafra. Neither the federal government nor Biafra had overwhelming military power, however, the federal government had international recognition, and tried to isolate Biafra internationally as a rebel force. Furthermore, they attempted to physically blockade Biafra.[9]

Immediately after the start of the war, the ICRC worked on prisoner investigations and support for local Red Cross societies. Subsequently, they began humanitarian aid to civilians in parallel. However, when a large-scale famine occurred in Biafra due to the federal government's blockade and the Biafra government's political use of the humanitarian crisis, this response became the focus of their activities.[10] In the summer of 1968, as soon as photos of children dying of starvation in Biafra appeared

---

[8] Philippe Sands, *East West Street: On the Origins of Genocide and Crimes against Humanity* (London: Weidenfeld & Nicolson, 2016); Samantha Power, *A Problem from Hell* (London: Harper Perennial, 2010), Part 4.

[9] John Stremlau, *The International Politics of the Nigerian Civil War, 1967–1970* (Princeton: Princeton University Press, 1977), 29–80; Lasse Heerten, *The Biafran War and Postcolonial Humanitarianism: Spectacles of Suffering* (Cambridge: Cambridge University Press, 2017), 44–82.

[10] Marie-Luce Desgrandchamps, "'Organiser à l'avance l'imprévisible': la guerre Nigéria-Biafra et son impact sur le CICR," *Revue internationale de la Croix-Rouge* 94, no. 888 (2012): 226.

in the Western media, the war attracted worldwide attention, and the pressure on the ICRC suddenly increased.[11]

The fact that this famine was often discussed in connection with Auschwitz also broadened interest. At that time, the perception that the Holocaust is a representative example of humanitarian crisis was also in the process of being formed.[12] While the famine was actually occurring, the Biafra government hired foreign advertising agencies, among other strategies, to enhance its legitimacy in the international community.[13]

The ICRC attempted to establish an airlift route to bring aid supplies to Biafra, but the federal government became hostile to the ICRC, suspecting it of smuggling weapons. Eventually, the federal government launched a military attack on the ICRC, resulting in casualties among its staff.[14] Among those active on the ground were Bernard Kouchner and others who would later establish Doctors Without Borders in France. On the ground, there was a growing call to publicize the severe famine in Biafra and the problems with the federal government to the international community. However, while the ICRC headquarters protested to the Nigerian federal government, it did not publicly criticize the government's actions.[15] Thus, a rift gradually emerged between the ICRC headquarters and the field. Upon returning to France, Kouchner and his colleagues spoke to Le Monde about their experiences in Biafra.[16] They then established the Committee Against the Biafra Genocide.

North Yemen Civil War

Similarly, in the North Yemen Civil War that occurred in the 1960s, the ICRC's attitude was again questioned. In 1962, Ahmad bin Yahya, the ruler of Yemen, died, and a group of elites and military personnel seized power, establishing the Yemen Arab Republic (North Yemen). They immediately requested support from Egypt and accepted the dispatch of troops from Egypt, but regions that resented the new regime

---

[11] Ibid., 229.

[12] Lasse Heerten, ""A" as in Auschwitz, "B" as in Biafra: The Nigerian Civil War, Visual Narratives of Genocide, and the Fragmented Universalization of the Holocaust," in *Humanitarian Photography: A History*, ed. H. Fehrenbach and D. Rodogno (New York: Cambridge University Press, 2015); Daniel Navon, ""We Are a People, One People": How 1967 Transformed Holocaust Memory and Jewish Identity in Israel and the US," *Journal of Historical Sociology* 28, no. 3 (September 2015).

[13] Stremlau, *International Politics*, 68, 110–17.

[14] Marie-Luce Desgrandchamps, "Revenir sur le mythe fondateur de Médecins sans frontières: les relations entre les médecins français et le cicr pendant la guerre du Biafra (1967–1970)," *Relations Internationales*, no. 146 (2011): 100–102.

[15] Ibid.

[16] This was against the ICRC's confidentiality rules, but the ICRC headquarters appreciated it and reprinted it in the journal that the ICRC regularly publishes. *Revue internationale de la Croix-Rouge* 51, no. 601 (1969): 15–21.

rebelled. The rebels received support from Saudi Arabia, and Britain, fearing Egypt's expansion of power, also joined in.[17]

In this war, various human rights violations were reported to the local representative of the Red Cross, but as of 1965, the ICRC headquarters wrote to the local representative that "the role of an ICRC delegate doesn't consist of investigation upon complaints relating to violations of human rights, but to practically assist the victims. Thank you for abstaining from verifying the information demanded of you."[18] Particularly, although the use of chemical weapons by the Egyptian army was questioned, the ICRC maintained silence. In 1967, when attacks on civilians, including humanitarian aid organizations, intensified, the ICRC finally issued a statement condemning such acts.[19]

There was increasing pressure to change the ICRC's policy of refusing to testify. As will be discussed later, in the 1970s, human rights abuses by authoritarian regimes in Central and South America became an issue, and calls for clarification of the facts intensified. From the late 1980s, historical verification of the ICRC's silence during the Holocaust began, and at the same time, criticism of the ICRC by activists such as Kouchner became more pronounced.[20]

The change that occurred in the 1960s was that in post-colonial armed conflicts, the premise of traditional ICRC-style humanitarian aid activities became difficult to establish. The ICRC assumed that sovereign states would manage their own armies and wage war and that there would be a neutral political space (at least in discourse) recognized by sovereign states, and recognition for activities to care for the wounded and sick without discrimination. However, in post-colonial armed conflicts, the subject was not always a sovereign state, with conflicts often bordering on regions and ethnicities. Therefore, the targets of attack were specific ethnicities or regions, and the distinction between soldiers/civilians was not clear. On the contrary, there were cases where general citizens of specific regions or ethnicities were intentionally targeted. Neutral political space was not always recognized, and humanitarian aid to the general public became difficult to distinguish from military support to specific forces. Therefore, the policy of refusing to testify to make humanitarian aid more effective was not always successful, and it led to criticism of bystanders to the massacre of the general public.

However, the primary purpose of the ICRC is to care for the injured. Testifying to large-scale human rights abuses and criticizing them in the international community can also endanger the aid activities themselves. The ICRC has won trust in conflict areas precisely because it has maintained a position of not siding with either side,

---

[17] Ginny Hill, *Yemen Endures: Civil War, Saudi Adventurism and the Future of Arabia* (Oxford: Oxford University Press, 2017), 9–32; Asher Orkaby, "The Yemeni Civil War: The Final British-Egyptian Imperial Battleground," *Middle Eastern Studies* 51, no. 2 (2015).

[18] Cited in Hill, *Yemen Endures*, 32.

[19] ICRC, *Annual Report 1967* (Geneva, 1968), 15–17.

[20] For criticism by Kouchner, see, for example, Bernard Kouchner, *Charity Business* (Paris: Le Pré aux clercs, 1986), 214–17.

including refusing to testify.[21] Doctors Without Borders is also at risk of endangering their aid activities by testifying, and even they have been cautious about doing so.[22] This is where international NGOs, which are committed to investigating human rights abuses and violations of humanitarian law, come into play.

4.2 Testimonies and Struggles of NGOs

Changes in the 1970s

In the 1970s, changes began to occur gradually. First, in 1977, the Additional Protocols to the Geneva Conventions were adopted at an international conference, expanding the content of the Geneva Conventions. This was due to the realization through the struggle for colonial independence that there was a need to provide adequate legal protection to combatants and civilians in situations other than traditional interstate armed conflicts.

The 1949 Geneva Conventions are essentially based on interstate wars. For example, suppose anti-government forces emerge in a country and a civil war ensues. The anti-government forces then wage a guerrilla war. The treatment of guerrillas, if asked, falls under domestic criminal law, not international law, and they are considered traitors. Even though guerrillas are essentially combatants, if they become traitors, they cannot receive prisoner of war treatment. Similarly, the 1949 Fourth Geneva Convention is primarily structured with interstate wars in mind, though its common Article 3, which allowed for very ambiguous and polysemic interpretations, applied civilian protection to situations such as civil wars. In contrast, the two Additional Protocols of 1977 refined norms such as the protection of prisoners of war and civilians and stipulated that they also apply to liberation struggles from colonial rule and civil wars.[23]

Secondly, human rights activists and NGOs began to emerge from authoritarian regimes in countries such as Chile, Brazil, and Argentina, documenting and denouncing human rights abuses. These local activists and NGOs then connected with international NGOs like Amnesty International, forming a global network. According to Samuel Moyn, who wrote the intellectual history of human rights, the human rights movement represented by Amnesty became the driving force behind the rise of human rights norms in the 1970s by connecting grassroots movements globally, rather than

[21] For the ICRC's strategy, see Joe Cropp, *The Humanitarian Fix: Navigating Civilian Protection in Contemporary Wars* (Abingdon: Routledge, 2021).

[22] For the relationship between human rights movements in America and Central and South America, see Mark Philip Bradley, *The World Reimagined: Americans and Human Rights in the Twentieth Century* (Cambridge: Cambridge University Press, 2016), 156–225.

[23] Anthony Cullen, *The Concept of Non-International Armed Conflict in International Humanitarian Law* (Cambridge: Cambridge University Press, 2010); Giovanni Mantilla, *Lawmaking under Pressure: International Humanitarian Law and Internal Armed Conflict* (Ithaca: Cornell University Press, 2020).

making the UN the center of reform.[24] In 1977, Amnesty International won the Nobel Peace Prize for denouncing the repression of the people by the Pinochet regime in Chile.[25] This global human rights movement began to impose certain restrictions on military aid and other matters in the 1970s, bringing the issue of human rights protection into the debate on American policy in Central and South America,[26] and it is no coincidence that many statisticians and forensic scientists specializing in the generation of DAC began their careers in places like Argentina and Guatemala. The global human rights movement flourished greatly from the issues in Central and South America, leading to activities monitoring violations of humanitarian law.[27]

The rise of the human rights movement was also closely linked to the context of criticism against the communist regime of the USSR. In 1973, Soviet author Aleksandr Solzhenitsyn published *The Gulag Archipelago* in France, exposing the fate of those considered counter-revolutionaries in the USSR, which ignited a movement against totalitarianism in Europe and created an ideological void. Those who dreamed of communism needed a new moral issue, with the void filled by human rights norms.[28]

The Salvadoran Civil War of the 1980s

The Salvadoran Civil War of the 1980s was where NGOs and sovereign states seriously battled over violations of international humanitarian and human rights law. In El Salvador, located in Central America, a small number of landowners had monopolized the majority of wealth since the end of the nineteenth century, and the majority of peasants and workers were struggling with severe poverty. Even in the 1970s, social structural reform did not progress, and the space for political dialogue was reduced by violence. Although elections were held several times, the results were manipulated by military intervention and government operations, and citizen protests intensified. In response, right-wing forces connected with the government and militarily assassinated protesting citizens one after another.[29]

In March 1980, Archbishop Oscar Romero, a central figure in the reform movement, was assassinated, and more and more people joined the resistance movement.

---

[24] Samuel Moyn, *The Last Utopia: Human Rights in History* (Cambridge: Belknap, 2010), 129–30.

[25] P. W. Kelly, ""Magic Words": The Advent of Transnational Human Rights Activism in Latin America's Southern Cone in the Long 1970s," in *The Breakthrough: Human Rights in the 1970s*, ed. S. Moyn and J. Eckel (Philadelphia: University of Pennsylvania Press, 2013).

[26] C. W. Walldorf, *Just Politics: Human Rights and the Foreign Policy of Great Powers* (Ithaca: Cornell University Press, 2008), 74–111.

[27] For information on the connection between the human rights movement in the United States and Latin America, see Mark Philip Bradley, *The World Reimagined: Americans and Human Rights in the Twentieth Century* (Cambridge: Cambridge University Press, 2016), 156–225.

[28] Jan-Werber Muller, *Contesting Democracy: Political Ideas in Twentieth-Century Europe* (New Haven: Yale University Press, 2013), 209; Moyn, *The Last Utopia*, Ch. 4.

[29] Julie Mazzei, *Death Squads or Self-Defense Forces?* (Chapel Hill: University of North Carolina Press, 2009).

Various political organizations demanding reform came together to form the Democratic Revolutionary Front (FDR).[30] In mid-1981, guerrilla organizations gathered to form the Farabundo Marti National Liberation Front (FMLN), which received support from countries such as Cuba and Nicaragua.[31] As martial law was imposed and repression intensified, it eventually led to a long-term civil war. Many ordinary citizens were tortured and killed in this civil war.

The United States was also, in effect, a party to the conflict in El Salvador. From the Kennedy administration, it encouraged the strengthening of El Salvador's military capabilities as part of its anti-communist policy.[32] When the Reagan administration came into power, the United States began to fully support the Salvadoran government. In his policy towards El Salvador, Reagan prioritized military solutions over political ones. In February 1981, the Reagan administration issued a document titled "Communist Interference in El Salvador,"[33] and in January of the following year, it issued National Security Decision Directive 17, which called for an increase in military aid to El Salvador and support for the suppression of rebel forces receiving foreign aid.[34]

Military and economic aid exploded after the Reagan administration took office. The total amount of military aid in 1980 was about 600 million dollars, and the total amount of economic aid was about 580 million dollars, but by 1984, both military and economic aid had reached about 200 million dollars.[35] In addition, American military advisors were deeply involved in counter-insurgency activities, including the assassination of key figures.[36] The US government was aware that various human rights abuses in El Salvador during the conflict were committed by right-wing forces.[37]

The Emergence of Testifying NGOs, Formation of Networks

Even before the onset of large-scale armed conflict, the civil society of El Salvador was facing severe human rights abuses by the government and had begun to resist,

[30] Robert Armstrong, *El Salvador: The Face of Revolution* (Boston: South End Press, 1982), 149–55.

[31] E. J. Wood, *Insurgent Collective Action and Civil War in El Salvador* (Cambridge: Cambridge University Press, 2003), 122–23.

[32] Russel Crandall, *The Salvador Option: The United States in El Salvador, 1977–1992* (Cambridge: Cambridge University Press, 2016).

[33] U.S. Department of State, *Communist Interference in El Salvador*, Special Report No. 80, February 23, 1981.

[34] National Security Decision Directive on Cuba and Central America, January 4 (NSDD-17), http://fas.org/irp/offdocs/nsdd/nsdd-017.htm.

[35] Americas Watch, *El Salvador's Decade of Terror* (New Haven: Yale University Press, 1991), Appendix A, 141.

[36] Crandall, *The Salvador Option*, 188–90.

[37] Clifford Krauss, "U.S., Aware of Killings, Worked with Salvador's Rightists, Papers Suggest," *The New York Times*, November 9, 1993.

albeit modestly. NGOs emerged to record who was abducted and killed by the government forces and paramilitary organizations, and how these events unfolded, including Socorro Jurídico, the Salvadoran Human Rights Commission, and Tutela Legal.[38]

Among them, Socorro Jurídico was the main source of information for American newspapers and others. Socorro Jurídico was established in 1975 by Catholic lawyers and law students, and by the late 1970s, it officially became an organization of the Catholic Church.[39] Its initial purpose was to provide legal support to citizens (especially the poor) who needed legal relief, but gradually it became an organization that resisted human rights abuses by the authoritarian regime through judicial means, such as seeking the release of people who were unjustly detained.[40]

Roberto Cuellar, a representative of Socorro Jurídico, testified that he and Archbishop Romero defined the activities of this organization as follows:

- An examination and analysis of the facts as well as reality;
- A study and rigorous interpretation of the rights that are violated and the Political Constitution;
- Exhausting all available legal resources and dialogue as part of a just solution; and
- Formulation of public accusations that could not be denied by the government nor the official justice system, as supported above all by formal testimonies from victims and vigorous as well as scrupulous investigations.[41]

Thus, from its inception, this organization attempted to resist human rights abuses by making full use of the weapon of the judicial system, because domestic law clearly stipulated human rights norms.

However, when Archbishop Romero, a central figure in the reform movement, was assassinated in March 1980, the armed conflict intensified along with the government's repression, and Socorro Jurídico could no longer resist within the domestic judicial system. With the enactment of Decree 507 in December 1980 (and further Decree 50 in February 1984), all proper legal procedures were halted, and the discretion of the security sector began to dominate. Furthermore, judicial officials who were inconvenient for the government or the military were also killed one after another.[42]

From this point on, the activities of Socorro Jurídico focused on the creation of records and reports of incidents that seemed to be human rights violations as the last remaining means of resistance.[43] They tried to keep a record of the fact of civilian killings. However, all local NGOs continued to receive intense pressure and interference from the Salvadoran and US governments. For example, two representatives

---

38 T.B. Jabine and R.P. Claude, eds., *Human Rights and Statistics* (Philadelphia: University of Pennsylvania Press, 1992), 100–102.

39 Americas Watch, *U.S. Reporting on Human Rights in El Salvador: Methodology at Odds with Knowledge* (New York: Americas Watch, 1982 June), 13.

40 Oscar Romero, *A Shepherd's Diary*, trans. Irene B. Hodgson (London: CAFOD, 1993), 19, 360.

41 Roberto Cuéllar with a response by Rev. R. S. Pelton, "The Legal Aid Heritage of Oscar Romero," in Rev. Robert S. Pelton et al., *Archbishop Romero and Spiritual Leadership in the Modern World* (Maryland: Lexington Books, 2015), 150.

42 Americas Watch, *El Salvador's Decade of Terror*, 71–85.

43 Romero, *A Shepherd's Diary*, 15.

of the Salvadoran Human Rights Commission were assassinated by paramilitary organizations.[44]

Meanwhile, in the United States, organizations were born that accused the Salvadoran conflict of violating international law, such as Americas Watch. This organization was derived from Helsinki Watch, a non-governmental organization established in 1978 which was mainly working to improve the human rights situation in Central and Eastern Europe. Its purpose was to monitor whether the USSR and East European countries were complying with the Helsinki Declaration (1975), which included respect for human rights, and to support various civil society groups.

In 1980, upon witnessing the birth of the Reagan administration, Aryeh Neier, one of the central figures of Helsinki Watch, believed that there was a need to expand the human rights movement to countries other than those that signed the Helsinki Final Act. According to Neier, "[t]he Reagan election made it plain to the Helsinki Watch leadership that they had to broaden their mandate. That was because the new administration came into office intent on repudiating the human rights policy of the previous president, Jimmy Carter."[45] He thought, "[i]f we wanted to have an impact on [US] human rights policy, we had to establish a capacity to work on Latin America."[46] In 1981, he established Americas Watch, an organization to monitor violations of international law in conflict zones and publicly denounce them, along with other activists.[47] They investigated and publicized the facts of violations of international humanitarian law and human rights abuses in cooperation with NGOs in El Salvador. Originally, Helsinki Watch adopted the method of "naming and shaming" governments that violate human rights through interactions with the media and government officials. Following this, Americas Watch also attempted to put pressure on the US and Salvadoran governments using this method.

The Struggle Over Data on Armed Conflicts

The struggle over human rights abuses (and violations of humanitarian law) in the El Salvador conflict was primarily in American public opinion and Congress. The main reason, needless to say, was that the US government was supporting the Salvadoran government forces, the perpetrators of the human rights abuses. NGOs aimed to change US government policy, and on January 26, 1982, Americas Watch released a 275-page report on human rights abuses (especially civilian casualties) in the El Salvador conflict, appealing to American public opinion.[48] The report, based on

[44] Jabine and Claude, *Human Rights and Statistics*, 101.

[45] Aryeh Neier, *The International Human Rights Movement* (Princeton: Princeton University Press, 2012), 206.

[46] Aryeh Neier, *Taking Liberties: Four Decades in the Struggle for Rights* (New York: Public Affairs, 2003), 153.

[47] Ibid., 166–67.

[48] Americas Watch Committee, *Report on Human Rights in El Salvador* (Washington, D. C.: The Union, 1982). The release of the report was also reported in newspapers. David Shribman, "Two Groups in U.S. Contend El Salvador Violates Civil Rights," *The New York Times*, January 27, 1982; John M. Goshko, "ACLU Criticizes El Salvador Over Human Rights Record," *The Washington Post*, January 27, 1982.

the findings of Socorro Jurídico, revealed that more than 10,000 civilians had been killed by the Salvadoran government by 1981. There was a reason why the report was released at this time. Two days later, President Reagan was scheduled to report on the human rights situation in El Salvador to Congress, which was based on the International Security and Development Cooperation Act of 1981, which required accountability for ensuring that aid was not promoting unjust human rights abuses. Nevertheless, Reagan stated in Congress as planned that the human rights situation in El Salvador was improving in line with international standards. He also claimed that Salvadoran NGOs were conducting biased investigations in favor of the guerrillas, and that their reports lacked credibility. From Reagan's response, it can be inferred that not only NGOs but also the US government seemed to care about international humanitarian law to some extent.

In response, Americas Watch argued how negligent the US government's information gathering was and how fair Socorro Jurídico's investigation methods were. According to them, Socorro Jurídico verified eyewitness testimonies, interviews with victims' relatives, and any available physical evidence on the ground, and wrote the report. The US government claimed that Socorro Jurídico was unreliable because it concealed its sources, but this was inevitable to ensure the safety of the informants. The US government's investigation relied on the report of the US ambassador to El Salvador, which in turn relied solely on reports from Salvadoran newspapers. However, all newspapers except for two that supported the right-wing and the government were closed, effectively just regurgitating government information. The US ambassador was not given the personnel or authority to conduct a full-scale investigation. Comparing the two, it was clear which was fairer, Americas Watch argued.[49]

Afterwards, the nature of investigations by human rights NGOs in El Salvador changed. The Catholic Church in El Salvador established the organization Tutela Legal for human rights investigations, and began to investigate and publicize human rights abuses by both the government and guerrillas.[50] Similarly, Americas Watch also began to report on human rights abuses by both sides from their 1983 report.[51] This was necessary to show as much as possible that the descriptions of human rights abuses were objective and neutral, in order to resist the tactics of the American and Salvadoran governments to dismiss everything as propaganda (later UN investigations found that human rights abuses by the government forces were overwhelmingly more numerous than those by the guerrillas[52]). Also, the interpretation of international law that was applied gradually became more sophisticated. For example, in a report jointly released by Americas Watch and the International Human Rights Law Group in April 1984, it discussed in detail how the Second Additional Protocol to

[49] Americas Watch, *U.S. Reporting on Human Rights.*

[50] Americas Watch, *El Salvador's Decade of Terror*, 121.

[51] Americas Watch and ACLU, *Third Supplement to the Report on Human Rights in El Salvador* (New York: Americas Watch Committee, 1983).

[52] The Commission on the Truth for El Salvador, *From Madness to Hope: The 12-year War in El Salvador* (April 1993).

the Geneva Conventions of 1977 and Common Article 3 of the Geneva Conventions of 1949 were applied.[53] This was a change not seen in previous reports.

The struggle by these NGO networks did not necessarily stop or significantly modify the human rights abuses by the American government's intervention policy and the Salvadoran government. However, as a result of international humanitarian law and human rights norms becoming major issues, it became more difficult for the major powers to commit human rights abuses, and they were forced to justify and proceed in various situations. Since the 1980s, Human Rights Watch has expanded its activities worldwide, investigating and publicizing various human rights issues and violations of humanitarian law.

4.3 Initiation of Fact-Finding by the United Nations

Today, not only NGOs but also UN organizations conduct fact-finding on armed conflicts. When did the UN start investigating and publicizing information about violations of humanitarian law? The UN is a universal international organization established in 1945, working to realize peace in the international community. However, the UN does not have a permanent organization that makes monitoring the implementation of international humanitarian law a major activity. The same was true for the League of Nations (LN), which existed before the UN. This is despite the fact that both the UN and the LN had functions to collect various information.

Incidentally, after World War I, a proposal was made within the Red Cross to establish the international committee, which would conduct investigations into violations of humanitarian law during wartime from a neutral standpoint, but this did not come to fruition.[54] The 1977 Additional Protocols to the Geneva Conventions stipulated the establishment of an International Fact-Finding Commission to investigate violations of humanitarian law (Article 90 of the First Additional Protocol), but this organization has yet to operate in an actual armed conflict.[55]

The violation of international humanitarian law has not been completely ignored. At the United Nations, the Secretary-General can conduct fact-finding investigations through special representatives for specific conflicts and human rights issues. Also, there are organizations within the UN that oversee international human rights law, and these human rights-related organizations partially undertake the monitoring of the implementation of humanitarian law. Specifically, the UN Commission on

---

[53] Lawyers Committee for International Human Rights and Americas Watch, *El Salvador's Other Victims: The War on the Displaced* (New York: April 1984), 183–97.

[54] Mark Lewis, *The Birth of the New Justice: the Internationalization of Crime and Punishment, 1919–1950* (Oxford: Oxford University Press, 2014), 91.

[55] Regarding the establishment of the International Fact-Finding Commission, see Frits Kalshoven, 'The International Humanitarian Fact-Finding Commission: its Birth and Early Years," in *Reflections on International Law from the Low Countries in Honour of Paul de Waat*, ed. Erik Denters and Nico Schrijver (The Hague: Martinus Nijhoff Publishers, 1998).

Human Rights (CHR) has been conducting fact-finding investigations on humanitarian law from the beginning of its activities, and has accumulated institutional practices over a long period of time. As will be mentioned later, the CHR was restructured into the Human Rights Council in 2006, and continues to investigate violations of humanitarian law in various armed conflicts.

However, unlike NGOs, the UN is an organization established by agreements between nations and is also a forum where governments negotiate. Therefore, it is exceptional for the UN to enter into conflict with sovereign states over DAC. Especially during the Cold War, the room for the UN to act freely was very limited in the gap between the US and the Soviet Union. Nevertheless, the CHR conducted fact-finding investigations on humanitarian law in the 1960s.

Before getting into the specifics of the background to this, the kind of organization the Commission on Human Rights (CHR) is needs to be examined. This organization was established in 1946 by the UN Economic and Social Council (ECOSOC), initially composed of 18 countries, but later increasing to 21 (1962), 32 (1967), 43 (1980), and 53 (1992) as the number of sovereign states increased due to decolonization.[56] Initially, the CHR did not have the authority to deal with individual cases of human rights violations by states. However, ECOSOC Resolution 1235 (XLII) of 1967 granted it the authority to conduct public deliberations on countries suspected of human rights violations.[57] Furthermore, in 1970, according to ECOSOC Resolution 1503 (XLVIII), it became possible to hold non-public deliberations on human rights violations in specific regions based on reports from individuals and NGOs. Resolution 1235 (XLII) is considered the basis for the Special Procedures by the CHR[58] who through these special procedures, was able to appoint individuals (Special Rapporteurs, or Independent Experts), or Working Groups composed of five members, to conduct investigations and reports.

The Issue of Israeli Occupied Territories Due to the Third Arab–Israeli War

The fact-finding of wars by the CHR began in the 1960s, with the trigger as the issue of occupied territories caused by the Third Arab–Israeli War. Behind the realization of this was the change in the United Nations due to decolonization. At the establishment of the United Nations in 1945, there were 51 member countries, but by 1965, after the decolonization of Asia and Africa, this had increased to 117 countries. As a result, in the United Nations General Assembly, the opinions of Asian and African countries became more accepted, and the International Convention on the Elimination of All Forms of Racial Discrimination (ICERD) was adopted at the twentieth United Nations General Assembly in 1965. The number of countries in the CHR, which

---

[56] Nazila Ghanea, "From UN Commission on Human Rights to UN Human Rights Council: One Step Forwards or Two Steps Sideways?" *International & Comparative Law Quarterly* 55, no. 3 (July 2006): 695.

[57] Howard Tolley Jr., *The U.N. Commission on Human Rights* (New York: Routledge, 2019 [1987]), 58.

[58] Ingrid Nifosi, "The UN Special Procedures in the Field of Human Rights. Institutional History, Practice and Conceptual Framework," *Deusto Journal of Human Rights*, no. 2 (December 2017), 132–34.

was 18 in 1946, expanded to 32 in 1967, and here, too, Asian and African countries became dominant.[59] Along with this change, from 1966 to 1979, nearly 20% of the agenda of the CHR was occupied by the issue of racial discrimination.[60]

Amidst the significant changes in the nature of the UN, in June 1967, the Third Arab–Israeli War broke out. The tension between Israel and Egypt, as well as Syria, rapidly escalated, leading to a full-scale armed conflict due to a surprise attack by Israel. Egypt, up until the brink of the armed conflict, had been taking actions that could be described as provocative, such as mobilizing troops to the Sinai Peninsula, requesting the withdrawal of the first United Nations Emergency Force, and blockading the Strait of Tiran, but once the war began, they were quickly defeated by the Israeli military.[61] As a result, Israel occupied the Sinai Peninsula and Gaza Strip, which were governed by Egypt, East Jerusalem and the West Bank under Jordan's control, and the Golan Heights, which were owned by Syria.

This occupation became the trigger for an investigation into violations of the Geneva Conventions at the CHR because the UN received information that the residences of Arab people living in these occupied territories were being destroyed one after another by the Israeli military. Immediately after the end of the armed conflict, Resolution 237 was adopted by the Security Council, calling for the protection of civilians and prisoners of war.[62] The following month, Secretary-General U Thant dispatched Nils Gussing as a special representative to the Middle East.[63]

This occupation by Israel was linked to colonialism and racism in the international community, with this trend symbolized by the International Conference on Human Rights held in Tehran in April 1968. Asian and African countries attempted to reinterpret the concept of human rights through this conference, arguing that poverty and development were the most important issues in human rights norms, and reinterpreting liberation from colonial rule as part of human rights.

The adopted resolution called for the need to ensure the fulfillment of human rights and humanitarian law in armed conflicts over decolonization.[64] This led to the convening of the diplomatic conference from 1974 to 1977, which established the first and second additional protocols to the Geneva Conventions. As mentioned earlier, the content of the 1949 Geneva Conventions was applied to colonial independence struggles and civil wars by these additional protocols.

---

[59] The seats by region were eight for Africa, six for Asia, four for Eastern Europe, six for Latin America, and eight for Western Europe and others (Tolley, *The U.N. Commission on Human Rights*, 32, 56–57).

[60] Jack Donnelly, "Human Rights at the United Nations 1955–85: The Question of Bias," *International Studies Quarterly* 32, no. 3 (1988): 283.

[61] For the Third Arab–Israeli War, see Wm. Roger Louis, and Avi Shlaim, eds., *The 1967 Arab–Israeli War: Origins and Consequences* (Cambridge: Cambridge University Press, 2012).

[62] S/RES/237, 14 June 1967.

[63] S/8158 and A/6797, 15 September 1967, para. 2.

[64] *Final Act of the International Conference on Human Rights* (Teheran, 22 April to 13 May 1968) (New York: United Nations, 1968), Resolution XXIII.

At this international conference, the issue of occupation by Israel was understood as a problem continuous with colonialism and racism.[65] One of the adopted resolutions called for the protection of civilians in the territories occupied during the Third Arab–Israeli War, based on the 1949 Geneva Conventions.[66] Thus, the issue of the occupied territories became one of the top priorities of Asian and African countries. However, issues such as civilian casualties in the Biafra conflict were not addressed at all at this international conference[67]; the third world countries that participated in this international conference were not interested in all conflicts and human rights issues. There were choices along their political interests.

The results of the Tehran Conference were reflected in several UN resolutions. For example, on December 19, 1968, General Assembly Resolution 2443 (XXIII) was adopted, deciding to establish a special investigation committee composed of three countries on the territories occupied in the Third Arab–Israeli War.[68] Furthermore, in March of the following year, the CHR established a special working group of experts on this issue[69] which was composed of diplomats and international law experts from countries such as Senegal, Austria, India, Yugoslavia, Peru, and Tanzania. They had already had experience investigating human rights issues in Southern Africa, centered on apartheid, in a working group of the CHR in March 1967.[70] At that time, the issue of the apartheid regime was a recurring theme in the General Assembly and the CHR, along with the Palestinian issue.

In January 1970, a report by the special working group was published. The purpose of the working group was to examine whether the 1949 Geneva Conventions could be applied to the occupied territories, and whether the protection of civilians stipulated in its Fourth Convention was being observed by Israel. Therefore, the expert team conducted interviews with a total of 103 people in various places, including visiting refugee camps in Jordan, in addition to analyzing related documents.[71] The conclusion of the report was that the 1949 Geneva Conventions applied to the occupied territories, and that there was evidence of violation of the Fourth Convention.[72] However, the special working group was not in a position to determine legal interpretations, and the conclusion of this report was considered merely an opinion.

Israel denied the legitimacy of the investigation by this special working group. They claimed that the decision of the CHR was based on the organized votes of Arab

---

[65] Roland Burke, *Decolonization and the Evolution of International Human Rights* (Philadelphia: University of Pennsylvania Press, 2010), 101–102; Steven L.B. Jensen, *The Making of International Human Rights: The 1960s, Decolonization, and the Reconstruction of Global Values* (Cambridge: Cambridge University Press, 2016), 189. In 1975, it was declared in United Nations General Assembly Resolution 3379 that "zionism is a form of racism and racial discrimination" (A/RES/3379).

[66] *Final Act of the International Conference on Human Rights*, 5.

[67] Burke, *Decolonization and the Evolution of International Human Rights*, 110.

[68] Subsequently, Ceylon, Somalia, and Yugoslavia were nominated.

[69] E/CN.4/RES/6 (XXV), March 4, 1969.

[70] E/CN.4/1111, February 1, 1973, 2.

[71] E/CN.4/1016, January 20, 1970, Introduction, para. 18–19.

[72] E/CN.4/1016/Add. 2, February 11, 1970, Conclusions, para. 1.

countries and pro-Arab countries within the committee, was for anti-Israel propaganda, and refused to cooperate with the investigation.[73] In 1971, the Israeli government decided to withhold its response to the applicability of the Fourth Convention for the time being.[74] The application of the Geneva Conventions to occupied territories implies the determination of territorial boundaries that should not be defined, which is because it could imply that countries like Egypt and Jordan holds sovereignty over these regions.[75]

Since then, the CHR has repeatedly addressed the issue of territories occupied by Israel, but each time, pro-Israel countries such as Israel and the United States have claimed that the issue set by the CHR is anti-Israel propaganda.[76] Indeed, violations of humanitarian law by Israel were a major issue, but it was also a major problem that the CHR did not sufficiently address cases of human rights violations other than apartheid and Palestine.

The Commission on Human Rights in the 1980s

The issues that the CHR dealt with were not only the Third Arab–Israeli War. The conflict in El Salvador, which was discussed in the previous section, was one of them. In 1980, the United Nations General Assembly raised the issue of human rights violations in El Salvador and asked the CHR to investigate. The CHR, in turn, appointed Spanish jurist Jose Antonio Pastor Ridruejo as a special representative to conduct a fact-finding mission.[77]

First, he conducted interviews mainly with government officials in El Salvador, and he also met with NGO officials investigating human rights abuses in Mexico and the United States.[78] In 1982, he submitted a report on the human rights situation. His term as a special representative was extended, and reports based on regular interviews were submitted. In a report submitted to the General Assembly in 1987, facts were published about acts that may violate international humanitarian law (especially the 1977 Additional Protocol), such as civilian casualties caused by bombing by the Salvadoran army.[79] These fact-finding missions by the special representative relied heavily on information from the NGO network discussed in the previous section.

In addition to the conflict in El Salvador, the CHR also conducted investigative activities in response to the Soviet invasion of Afghanistan in 1979. About four years after the invasion by the Soviet Union, the Soviets intensified air strikes against villages believed to be supporting anti-government forces, which was a strategy to

[73] E/CN.4/1016, January 20, 1970, Ch. 1, para. 22.

[74] Esther Rosalind Cohen, *Human Rights in the Israeli-occupied Territories, 1967–1982* (Manchester: Manchester University Press, 1985), 44.

[75] Ibid., 44–45.

[76] Sarah Joseph and Eleanor Jenkin, "The United Nations Human Rights Council: Is the United States Right to Leave This Club?" *American University International Law Review* 35, no. 1 (2019).

[77] E/CN.4/1502, January 18, 1982.

[78] E/CN.4/1502, January 18, 1982, para. 8–9.

[79] A/41/710, January 9, 1987.

eliminate anti-government forces.[80] As a result, with the rapid increase in the number of victims, in March 1984, a recommendation was finally made at the Economic and Social Council to appoint a special rapporteur on the human rights situation in Afghanistan, and a public investigation into violations of humanitarian law began.[81] At this time, a problem at the CHR was that there was little investigation and criticism of the human rights situation in Eastern countries, especially that sufficient investigation was not conducted on Poland, where martial law was imposed in 1981,[82] with the fact-finding in Afghanistan a valuable case that differed from such trends of the UN.

In February of the following year, 1985, a report on the human rights situation in Afghanistan was released. The special rapporteur was Felix Ermacora, an expert on human rights in Austria, who conducted interviews with relevant organizations and individuals about the human rights situation in Afghanistan and collected information. He asked the Afghanistan government for cooperation to conduct a local survey, but they refused to cooperate, saying that there was no problem with the human rights situation. The Afghanistan government, and even the Soviet Union, claimed that the fact-finding by the CHR was an interference in domestic affairs.[83] Therefore, it was not possible to conduct a local survey in Afghanistan, and instead he conducted a survey in Pakistan and collected the necessary information.

The report concluded that in this conflict, there were abuses of prisoners of war, deliberate attacks on women and children, bombings and massacres of civilians, use of poison gas, and retaliations and terrorism, all of which were violations of international humanitarian law.[84] After this report, fact-finding reports on the Afghanistan War were released every year, and the investigation activities continued even after the Soviet withdrawal.

Establishment of the UN High Commissioner for Human Rights

Along with the CHR, the Office of the United Nations High Commissioner for Human Rights (OHCHR) has been monitoring violations of humanitarian law in wars. The UN High Commissioner for Human Rights was recommended for establishment in the Vienna Declaration and Programme of Action adopted at the World Conference on Human Rights in June 1993, and was established by General Assembly Resolution 48/141 in December of the same year, after lobbying by various NGOs and the US government.[85] In line with this, the OHCHR, led by the United Nations High Commissioner for Human Rights, was established.

---

[80] Larry P. Goodson, "Periodicity and intensity in the Afghan War," *Central Asian Survey* 17, no. 3 (1998): 476; William Maley, *The Afghanistan Wars* (London: Red Globe Press, 2020), 40.

[81] Tolley, *The U.N. Commission on Human Rights*, 130–31.

[82] Richard Bernstein, "U.N. Rights Study Finds Afghan Abuses by Soviet," *The New York Times*, March 1, 1985.

[83] E/CN.4/1985/21, February 19, 1985, para. 27–32.

[84] E/CN.4/1985/21, February 19, 1985, para. 97–119.

[85] A/RES/48/141, January 7, 1994; Thomas G. Weiss, David P. Forsythe, Roger A. Coate, and Kelly-Kate Pease, *The United Nations and Changing World Politics* (8th Edition) (New York: Routledge, 2020), 211.

The idea of setting up a High Commissioner for Human Rights has actually existed since just after World War II, however, it took a very long time to realize. First, in 1947, one of the drafters of the Universal Declaration of Human Rights proposed it, but it did not come to fruition. Then, in the 1960s, NGOs called for the establishment of a High Commissioner, and it was discussed in the CHR, but again it did not materialize. Finally, at the 1993 World Conference on Human Rights, the establishment was proposed again in the Vienna Declaration, and it was realized by a resolution of the United Nations General Assembly.[86]

The OHCHR played a role in supporting the Special Rapporteurs and Working Groups appointed by the CHR. Also, the OHCHR is obligated to submit activity reports to the CHR and the General Assembly, and has conducted investigative reports on human rights situations around the world. In the examples of war data generation seen in the following chapters, the OHCHR appears as a main actor, expected to stop human rights violations (and violations of humanitarian law) through negotiation and dialogue. At the same time, it is also desired to publicly protest against countries that have committed human rights violations (and violations of humanitarian law) as necessary.[87]

Restructuring to the Human Rights Council and the Establishment of the International Criminal Court

Now, let us return to the Commission on CHR once more. As the 2000s began, criticism grew that the investigations by the CHR were biased towards certain regions and issues, such as Palestine, and it was decided to restructure the CHR into the Human Rights Council. In 2004, UN reform was proposed in the report "A More Secure World: Our Shared Responsibility," and it was stated that the CHR also needed reform. In 2005, Secretary-General Kofi Annan criticized the CHR in his speech as follows:

> The Commission in its current form has some notable strengths. It can take action on country situations. It can appoint rapporteurs and other experts. And it works closely with civil society groups.
>
> At the same time, the Commission's ability to perform its tasks has been overtaken by new needs, and undermined by the politicization of its sessions and the selectivity of its work. We have reached a point at which the Commission's declining credibility has cast a shadow

[86] Theo Van Boven, "The United Nations High Commissioner for Human Rights: The History of a Contested Project," *Leiden Journal of International Law* 20, no. 4 (December 2007); Julie Mertus, *The United Nations and Human Rights: A Guide for a New Era* (London: Routledge, 2005), 8–36; William A. Schabas, "The United Nations High Commissioner for Human Rights and International Humanitarian Law," in *Strengthening Measures for the Respect and Implementation of International Humanitarian Law and Other Rules Protecting Human Dignity in Armed Conflict, 28th Round Table on Current Problems of International Humanitarian Law, Sanremo, 2–4 September 2004*, ed. International Institute of Humanitarian Law (Sanremo: International Institute of Humanitarian Law, 2004), 196–97.

[87] Felice D. Gaer and Christen L. Broecker, "Introduction," in *The United Nations High Commissioner for Human Rights*, ed. Felice D. Gaer and Christen L. Broecker (Leiden: Martinus Nijhoff Publishers, 2014), 6.

on the reputation of the United Nations system as a whole, and where piecemeal reforms will not be enough.[88]

In March 2006, the Human Rights Council was established by General Assembly Resolution 60/251. The Council inherited most of its functions and powers from the CHR, but it gained the ability to conduct the Universal Periodic Review, which reviews the human rights records of all UN member states every four years. The Council is composed of 47 countries, which are elected by secret ballot at the UN General Assembly. The member states are selected in a certain number from each region, divided into groups such as the Africa Group, Asia Group, Latin America and Caribbean Group, Eastern Europe, Western Europe and others.

In this way, human rights-related organizations such as the CHR and OHCHR have been active in the UN's monitoring of the implementation of international humanitarian law. In the 1990s, the International Criminal Court joined this network, with examples of international criminal trials including the International Military Tribunal at Nuremberg and the International Military Tribunal for the Far East held after World War II. In these trials, crimes such as the killing and abuse of civilians during wartime were judged based on the Charter of the International Military Tribunal and the Charter of the International Military Tribunal for the Far East, which were agreed upon by the victorious nations.[89] These trials were mainly conducted based on evidence collected from documents. Also, in the Nuremberg Trials, testimonies of survivors of the Jewish genocide were considered important evidence.[90]

In 1993, in response to the conflict in the former Yugoslavia, the International Criminal Tribunal for the former Yugoslavia (ICTY) was established, and in 1994, in response to the civil war in Rwanda, the International Criminal Tribunal for Rwanda (ICTR) was established, each based on a United Nations Security Council resolution (the establishment and trials of the ICTY will be examined in Chaps. 5 and 6). Then, in 2002, the International Criminal Court (ICC) was established as a permanent international court to judge international crimes based on the Rome Statute. As a result, DAC is no longer just for "naming and shaming" the parties involved, but it is becoming increasingly important as a basis for pursuing legal responsibility.

*

The Geneva Conventions, established in 1949, initially had almost no system in place to monitor their enforcement. However, with the emergence of NGOs that investigate and expose human rights abuses, a global network was formed that also began to investigate and expose violations of international humanitarian law alongside human rights law. The rapid development of such humanitarian networks was

[88] U.N. Secretary-General, "Secretary-General's Address to the Commission on Human Rights" (April 7, 2005), https://www.un.org/sg/en/content/sg/statement/2005-04-07/secretary-generals-address-commission-human-rights.

[89] Annette Weinke, *The Nuremberg Trials*, trans. Takumi Itabashi (Tokyo: Chuokoron-Shinsha, 2015) [Japanese]; Yoshinobu Higurashi, *The Tokyo Trial* (Tokyo: Kodansha, 2008) [Japanese].

[90] *Sands, East West Street*, Chap. 126.

seen in the conflicts in Central and South America in the 1980s. In this chapter, we discussed the Salvadoran Civil War and the birth of Human Rights Watch as specific examples. The United Nations also developed a systematic function to investigate violations of humanitarian law along with human rights abuses, with this function carried out by the Commission on Human Rights, with the issue of occupied territories following the Third Arab–Israeli War being one of the early cases. Furthermore, the United Nations has increased its ability to investigate violations of humanitarian law through the establishment of the OHCHR and the reorganization from the CHR to the Human Rights Council. From the perspective of enforcing international humanitarian law, the establishment of the International Criminal Court was an extremely important event, because it led to the legal responsibility for violations of humanitarian law being pursued in court. However, with the establishment of such a system, strict war data that could serve as legal evidence became necessary. So, who has been generating such strict war data and how? In the next chapter, we will consider this issue.

Chapter 5
Counting the Dead: War and Statistics

Contents

When trying to understand war, the number of deaths often becomes a point of discussion. The more deaths there are, the larger and more intense the war is supposed to be. There is a saying, "The death of one man is a tragedy. The death of millions is a statistic,"[1] and there are aspects of war that can only be understood through statistics. This chapter focuses on several cases where humanitarian networks have collected civilian death data in opposition to the state and analyzed it using statistical methods. This will clarify the nature of statistical data and the structure of the humanitarian networks that generate it.[2]

---

[1] This phrase is often attributed to Stalin, but no evidence has been found that Stalin actually said it.

[2] For studies on statistical analysis of the number of war dead, see *Counting Civilian Casualties: An Introduction to Recording and Estimating Nonmilitary Deaths in Conflict*, ed. Taylor B. Seybolt, Jay D. Aronson, and Baruch Fischhoff (Oxford: Oxford University Press, 2013); Peter Andreas and Kelly M. Greehill, *Sex, Drugs, and Body Counts: The Politics of Numbers in Global Crime and Conflict* (Ithaca and London: Cornell University Press, 2010); Jana Asher, David Banks, and Fritz J. Scheuren, eds., *Statistical Methods for Human Rights* (New York; London: Springer, 2008), and others.

M. Igarashi, *War and Data on Armed Conflicts*, Evidence-Based Approaches to Peace and Conflict Studies 14, https://doi.org/10.1007/978-981-97-6418-1_5

5.1 Uncertain Numbers

Prehistory of War Statistics

The word "statistics" originates from the Latin word *status*. According to Olivier Rey, who wrote the history of statistics, this word *status* meant position or situation, but it could also refer to a form of government, while it also had the meaning of inventory.[3] This led to the word *Statistik* in Germany, which comprehensively describes the state of national governance, which became statistics or statistique. Later, these words came to mean a method of capturing the nature of a state or society through numbers. This chapter uses the word statistics in this sense of a method of capturing the nature of a state or society through numbers. The concept of statistical analysis became widespread in Europe in the nineteenth century. At the beginning of the nineteenth century, departments dealing with statistics were established as public institutions in countries such as Prussia, Britain, and France. Also, societies for studying statistics were created in various places, and the idea of statistics spread among the citizens. As a result, various statistical data were generated in areas such as population, poverty, and public health.[4]

The statistics on war that this book focuses on are closely related to the development of public health. As is well known, Florence Nightingale statistically analyzed the relationship between the deaths of British soldiers and the sanitary conditions in hospitals during the Crimean War (1853–1856), in which she herself served. In this war, the allied forces centered on France, the Ottoman Empire, and Britain, as well as the Kingdom of Sardinia, fought against Russia, causing significant damage to each of their armies. However, the major cause of the damage was not just the intensity of the battle, but also the inadequacy of the medical system and sanitary management.[5] Nightingale revealed the reality by statistically analyzing the documents of the British army, using her good understanding of mathematics, including statistics. Furthermore, it is said that William Farr, an epidemiologist who was active in the British population registration office, also cooperated with her investigation.[6] The collection of statistical data on war casualties significantly developed as a practice during World War I. As mentioned in the Chap. 2, all European countries tried to collect data on all soldiers' deaths during World War I. This attempt to collect data was extremely difficult, but it was the time when the state began to statistically grasp the number of war dead.

How were civilian casualties treated? In World War I, civilian casualties were almost ignored. As discussed in the Chap. 3, the norm of civilian protection was

---

[3] Olivier Rey, *When the World Became Number* (Paris: Desclée De Brouwer, 2021), 39.

[4] Ibid., Ch. 4–5. Also, Alain Desrosieres, *The Politics of Large Numbers: A History of Statistical Reasoning*, trans. Camille Naish (Cambridge: Harvard University Press, 1998), Ch. 5–6.

[5] Geoffrey Wawro, *Warfare and Society in Europe, 1792–1914* (Abingdon: Routledge, 2000), 60–61.

[6] Hugh Small, *A Brief History of Florence Nightingale and Her Real Legacy: A Revolution in Public Health* (London: Robinson, 2017), Ch. 3.

codified in the Fourth Geneva Convention of 1949 and gained the status of an international norm, however, this did not lead to the international institutionalization of a system to collect and publish data on civilian casualties. An important exception was the International Military Tribunal at Nuremberg, where the number of deaths among Jews, including civilian victims, was discussed.[7] As revealed in Chap. 4, it was not until the 1970s that humanitarian networks such as NGOs and international organizations began to collect and publish data on civilian casualties. And it was not until later that attempts were made to understand the full extent of war casualties, including civilians, through comprehensive statistical analysis.

Vietnam War

Before examining the origins of statistical analysis of civilian casualties, it is pertinent to consider the case of the Vietnam War. In this war, the US military tried to understand the situation and formulate appropriate strategies through statistics. However, the statistical data they collected was often flawed, leading to a failure to understand the situation and causing massive civilian casualties. What exactly happened?

The Vietnam War began as a struggle for Vietnam to break free from French colonial rule after World War II. In the process, Vietnam was divided into North and South, with the North under the communist regime led by Ho Chi Minh and the South becoming a French colony. North Vietnam began supporting the decolonization struggle in South Vietnam, forcing France to withdraw, however, the United States, fearing the spread of communism in Vietnam (and its neighboring countries), began to militarily support South Vietnam and intervene in the conflict. When military support for South Vietnam reached its limit, the United States began full-scale military intervention in the mid-1960s, leading to a quagmire of war.

For the US military, the Vietnam War was a war of attrition.[8] In other words, it was a war where geographical indicators were not useful in measuring the progress of the war. If it were a war to seize enemy territory, geographical expansion would be the goal, but the Vietnam War was not necessarily so. Instead of armies clashing head-on, it was a confrontation between regular armies and guerrillas. While struggling with the guerrillas' surprise attacks in unfamiliar Vietnam, the US military used the extent to which they could reduce the power of the guerrillas as a measure of progress. Many villages supported the guerrillas, providing them with information as well as food supplies and, therefore, the US military had to confront not only the guerrillas but also the social structure that supported them. This led to the deployment of counter-insurgency operations.

Counter-insurgency operations traditionally emphasize both military operations to physically attack guerrillas and political and economic policies to separate guerrillas from civilians. That is, while weakening the power of the guerrillas with military force, they offer a better life to the civilians, thereby reducing the legitimacy of

---

[7] William Seltzer, "Population Statistics, the Holocaust, and the Nuremberg Trials," *Population and Development Review* 24, no. 3 (September, 1998): 533–36.

[8] Christian G. Appy, *Working-Class War: American Combat Soldiers and Vietnam* (Chapel Hill: University of North Carolina Press, 1993), 153–54.

the guerrillas in the local society. However, at this time, the US military placed more emphasis on military operations than on political and economic policies. The representative operation was "search-and-destroy." This mission was to kill guerrillas one by one, which was renamed "sweeping operations" due to the bad impression and reputation of this name in 1968.[9] This was literally a campaign to kill guerrillas.

The body count, which counts the number of enemy and ally corpses, was used as an important indicator of military operations.[10] The term "body count" was officially used by the US military at the time[11] as an indicator based on the hypothesis that the more enemy soldiers were killed, the more the enemy's military power would decrease, and eventually lead to advantageous peace negotiations with North Vietnam.[12] William C. Westmoreland, who served as the commander of the US forces in Vietnam from 1964, said, "statistics were, admittedly, an imperfect gauge of progress, yet in the absence of conventional frontlines, how else to measure it?"[13] For the US military, the body count was one of the few clear and available statistical data.

Westmoreland presented the following data in his 1968 report and revealed his analysis (Fig. 5.1).

> The chart on the facing page shows the general upward trend in the ratio of friendly to enemy casualties. [...] The trend is clearly up, and at the present time it has reached a ratio in which six of the enemy are killed for each allied soldier lost. From a purely military standpoint this trend shows the impact of the introduction of U.S. troops, the steady improvement in performance by all allied forces, and the steady decline in battlefield performance by the enemy.[14]

What is shown here is a situation evaluation model that evaluates the war situation from the change in the number of North Vietnamese soldiers who died when one soldier of the allied forces, including the US military, died. The body count provided the basic data for this evaluation model. Robert S. McNamara, who served as Secretary of Defense during this period, also tried to understand the war situation in the

---

[9] James William Gibson, *The Perfect War: Technowar in Vietnam* (Boston: Atlantic Monthly Press, 1986), 187; Appy, *Working-Class War*, 156.

[10] However, the body count was just one of many indicators. For a comprehensive analysis of the indicators used by the US military in the Vietnam War, see Gregory A. Daddis, *No Sure Victory: Measuring U.S. Army Effectiveness and Progress in the Vietnam War* (New York: Oxford University Press, 2011).

[11] For details on the body count data at the time, refer to the following document. Thomas C. Thayer, ed., *A System Analysis View of the Vietnam War 1965–1972, Vol. 8 Casualties and Losses* (Washington, DC: Office of the Assistant Secretary of Defense, Programs Analysis and Evaluation, 1975).

[12] Robert S. McNamara and Brian VanDeMark, *In Retrospect: The Tragedy and Lessons of Vietnam* (New York: Times Books, 1995), 211.

[13] Quoted in Scott Sigmund Gartner and Marissa Edson Myers, "Body Counts and "Success" in the Vietnam and Korean Wars," *The Journal of Interdisciplinary History* 25, no. 3 (Winter, 1995), 379. However, progress evaluation by body count was also implemented in the Korean War.

[14] W. C. Westmoreland and U.S.G. Sharp, *Report on the War in Vietnam, as of 30 June 1968* (Washington, D.C.: U.S. Government Printing Office, 1968), 190–91. The original graph's line was drawn in red, but it was very hard to see, so it was changed to black.

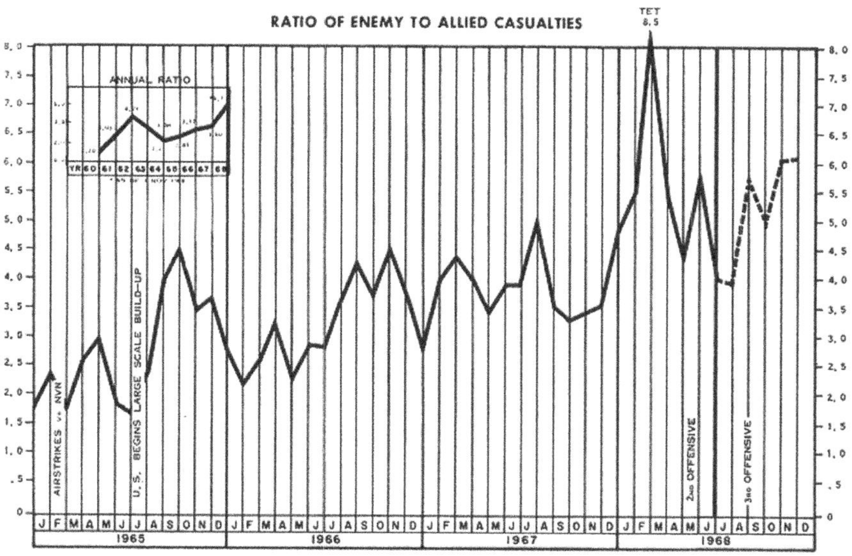

Fig. 5.1 Ratio of enemy to allied casualties

same way based on the data of the body count.[15] Furthermore, the body count was used not only to measure progress, but also as a number to promote competition within the military. A system was introduced where each unit would be relocated if it could not produce high numbers, with high numbers also required to get promotions or special leave.[16] This put pressure on each unit to produce high numbers.

The use of body counts to measure the state of the war was rooted in the ideology of numerical rationalism that was prevalent in the American government and military in the 1960s. The adherent of this ideology was McNamara, who believed that all phenomena could be accurately analyzed by being measured with objective numbers: in his own words, "I see quantification as a language to add precision to reasoning about the world."[17] He had accumulated the practice of numerical rationalism throughout his career. After graduating from Harvard Business School, he served as an assistant professor at the same university from 1940, but with the outbreak of World War II, he worked on the US Army's statistical management plan. After the war, he joined Ford and served as president. Then, in 1961, he became Secretary of Defense under J.F. Kennedy and carried out reforms at the Pentagon.[18]

McNamara's numerical rationalism ideology strongly resonated with the policy of the RAND Corporation, a think tank established after World War II for the purpose of

[15] McNamara and Brian VanDeMark, *In Retrospect*, 237–38.

[16] Gibson, *The Perfect War*, 112–20; Gunenter Lewy, *America in Vietnam* (New York: Oxford University Press, 1978), 81; Nick Turse, *Kill Anything That Moves: The Real American War in Vietnam* (New York: A Metropolitan Book, 2013), 43–45.

[17] McNamara and Brian VanDeMark, *In Retrospect*, 6.

[18] Ibid., 21–25.

strategic planning and research for the US military. Although it is an independent non-profit organization, many of its members entered the Department of Defense during the Vietnam War and exerted a great influence. This organization also conducted research and analysis based on the ideology of numerical rationalism, mainly on security issues, and contributed to policy formulation.[19]

Inflation of Numbers

The data from body counts was emphasized in policy and strategy formulation, but the numbers of body counts were inflated on the battlefield. The cause can be attributed to several factors, along with the intensification of competition within the military. First, each unit on the battlefield did not have the luxury of confirming and counting each body, and in many cases, they had to estimate. Especially in the case of air raids, ground confirmation work was almost impossible, and they reported approximate numbers. Furthermore, because each unit counted bodies independently, there were cases where one body was counted twice.[20] Under such circumstances, if the military had a motive to seek higher numbers, it would inevitably lead to inflation.

The biggest problem with data tampering was that civilians who were not armed and did not participate in combat were also counted as "Viet Cong" (guerrilla soldiers).[21] Nick Turse, who analyzed civilian casualties in the Vietnam War, explains this as follows:

> "Upon arrival," assistant machine gunner Robert Gray said later, "we found dead and wounded Vietnamese children." [...] In death, this small group of children had morphed into guerrillas and then into uniformed enemy soldiers as the body count wound its way through the military's statistics generation machine. [...] The practice of counting all dead Vietnamese as enemy kills became so pervasive that one of the most common phrases of the war was: "If it's dead and Vietnamese, it's VC."[22]

The American military killed civilians who should not have been killed, and fabricated higher numbers by turning them into guerrilla soldiers. Also, racial discrimination against Vietnamese people was rampant within the military, which also became a background for the normalization of civilian killings.[23]

Furthermore, there was a problem with the classification of deaths caused by air strikes. In the case of attacks in the "free-fire zones" set by the US military (renamed "specified strike zones" after 1965), everyone there was automatically considered a soldier, but in reality, they were not all soldiers. In the case of free-fire zones, warnings of air strikes were given to residents in advance, and it was assumed that there were no civilians. However, residents who refused to migrate for various reasons or could

---

[19] Alex Abella, *Soldiers of Reason: The Rand Corporation and the Rise of the American Empire* (Orlando: Harcourt, 2008).

[20] Lewy, *America in Vietnam*, 79.

[21] Gibson, *The Perfect War*, Ch. 5.

[22] Turse, *Kill Anything That Moves*, 46–47.

[23] Gibson, *The Perfect War*, 141–42, 181–82; Philip Knightley, *The First Casualty: The War Correspondent as Hero and Myth-Maker from the Crimea to Iraq* (Baltimore: The Johns Hopkins University Press, 2004), 423–28.

not read the warning documents became targets of attack.[24] Later, a subcommittee of the US Senate reported data that 30,000 non-combatants had died due to attacks in the "free-fire zones" by 1968.[25]

In this way, many units disguised civilians as combatants in body counts and fabricated data. As a result, the statistical data on enemy soldier deaths deviated greatly from reality. It was pointed out at the time that there was a large discrepancy between the data and reality. According to the official historical records of the US military, even within the military, there were continuous criticisms that the statistics of the South Vietnam Military Assistance Command underestimated the number of enemy soldiers and overestimated the number of enemy deaths.[26] Thomas C. Thayer, who led the analysis of statistical data in the Vietnam War, also stated in his book, "It is doubtful whether anybody, including Hanoi, really knows how many communist troops died."[27] And, "Considerable effort was made to check the validity of the communist loss estimates but the results were not conclusive."[28] As stated, the number of enemy soldiers killed was extremely uncertain data, contrary to the expectations of policy makers.

Deviation from Civilian Protection Norms

In the Vietnam War, body count was emphasized in data collection, but as can be seen from the falsification of data, there was little concern for civilian casualties; in fact, there was virtually no category of civilians in the body count. In the 1960s, there were norms for civilian protection under international law. As discussed in Chap. 3, the 1949 Geneva Conventions clearly stipulate the protection of civilians. Moreover, the US military ostensibly accepted the Geneva Conventions. In fact, when American soldiers arrived in Vietnam, they were given two pocket cards with the rules of engagement written on them, with one labeled "Nine Rule" and the other titled "The Enemy in Your Hands." The former stated that the US military should not be hostile to Vietnamese civilians and should not provoke their resentment, while the latter briefly described the treatment of prisoners of war as stipulated in the Geneva Conventions.[29] However, these provisions were often ignored on the ground.[30]

Apart from the provisions of international law, the 1962 edition of the US Army's *Field Service Regulations—Operations, FM100-5* also explained that in such guerrilla warfare, support from local civilians is important from a military strategy

---

[24] Lewy, *America in Vietnam*, 105; Gibson, *The Perfect War*, 135.

[25] Cecil B. Currey, "Free Fire Zones," in *The Encyclopedia of the Vietnam War: A Political, Social and Military History*, ed. Spencer Tucker (Santa Barbara, California: ABC-CLIO, 2011), 394–95.

[26] Graham A. Cosmas, *MACV: The Joint Command in the Years of Withdrawal, 1968–1973* (Washington, D.C.: U.S. Army Center of Military History, 2006), 86.

[27] Thomas C. Thayer, *War without Fronts: The American Experience in Vietnam* (Annapolis: Naval Institute Press, 1985), 101.

[28] Ibid., 102.

[29] Gibson, *The Perfect War*, 129–31.

[30] Ibid., 183–84.

perspective.[31] Since it is the local citizens who support the guerrillas, in irregular warfare, support from the citizens must be gained not through normal combat actions, but through political and economic policies (i.e., the provision of a better life). Therefore, indiscriminately killing local civilians was a major problem from a strategic perspective. According to the Pentagon Papers (an analysis record of the Vietnam War created by a group of researchers under the direction of McNamara from 1966), there was concern at the time that mass killing of civilians through air strikes could potentially damage America's image both domestically and internationally.[32] However, on the actual battlefield, many civilians were killed by large-scale air strikes and indiscriminate gunfire. Certainly, the cause of civilian deaths was not only due to military actions by the US forces, but also due to the South Vietnamese Liberation National Front.

How many civilians actually died as a result of the Vietnam War? Thomas C. Thayer states that there is no data on civilian casualties in US military statistics.[33] In the US military's body count, there was no category for civilians. Based on available data, Gunter Lewy, who estimated civilian casualties, argues that the number of civilian deaths was at least 40,000 to 60,000.[34] The Vietnamese government claims that a total of 2 million civilians died.[35]

Did the death of civilians due to US military actions not become an issue within the military? When Neil Sheehan, a reporter for *The New York Times*, asked Commander Westmoreland "if he was worried about the large number of civilian casualties from the air strikes and the shelling," he replied "Yes, Neil, it is a problem, [...] but it does deprive the enemy of the population, doesn't it?"[36] At that time, the massacre of civilians was slowly becoming a social issue due to the efforts of many journalists and whistleblowers, including Seymour Hersh. Among them, the massacre in the village of Son My (My Lai massacre) in 1968 had a great impact, where American soldiers massacred hundreds of unarmed, non-resistant Vietnamese residents, most of them children, women, and the elderly.[37]

---

[31] U.S. Department of the Army, *FM 100–5: Field Service Regulations - Operations, 1962* (Washington, United States Government Printing Office, 1962), 127–35.

[32] *The Pentagon Papers* (Gravel Edition) (Boston: Beacon Press, 1971), Vol. 4. Chapter I, "The Air War in North Vietnam, 1965–1968," 171–72.

[33] Thayer, *War Without Fronts*, 125.

[34] Lewy, *America in Vietnam*, 442–53.

[35] Turse, *Kill Anything That Moves*, 13.

[36] Neil Sheehan, *A Bright Shining Lie John Paul Vann and America in Vietnam* [Ebook] (New York: Vintage, 2009), 620.

[37] For the process of the incident becoming a social issue, see Knightley, *First Casualty*, 428–40. For details of the incident, see William Thomas Allison, My Lai: An American Atrocity in the Vietnam War (Baltimore: The Johns Hopkins University Press, 2012); Howard Jones, *My Lai: Vietnam, 1968, and the Descent into Darkness* (New York: Oxford University Press, 2017).

5.2 Estimating Deaths

Guatemalan Civil War

The counter-insurgency operations that the United States conducted in Vietnam were exported to civil wars in Central and South America through military support, leading to many civilian massacres. One of the representative examples was the civil war in Guatemala, however, unlike the Vietnam War, the number of victims of the massacre in this civil war has been scientifically investigated by statistical analysis. This statistical survey forms the basis for statistical analysis in various subsequent civil wars.

The Guatemalan Civil War began around 1960. Initially, government repression and opposition movements were small, but the conflict escalated with the birth of a military regime and the subsequent formation of leftist guerrillas. As intense repression by government forces and others unfolded in urban areas, the guerrillas lost their power and moved their base to local communities. In 1978, when General Romeo Lucas García assumed the presidency, a large-scale military operation, "Operation Ash," was executed. As a result, villages in the south and west were thoroughly destroyed. In 1982, Ríos Montt became president through a military coup, and attacks on civilians became even more intense. This conflict would ultimately continue until 1996, but it is said that the period from 1978 to 1983 had the most incidents of massacres.[38]

According to the report of the Comisión para el Esclarecimiento Histórico (CEH) of the Guatemalan Civil War, which will be mentioned later, the number of victims between 1960 and 1996 was estimated to be about 20,000.[39] The attacks were carried out indiscriminately against soldiers/civilians, and many of the victims were women and children. Also, 83% of the recorded victims were people of the Maya ethnicity, showing a bias based on racism.[40]

In the Guatemalan Civil War, as in the Salvadoran Civil War mentioned in Chap. 4, countless brutal human rights abuses occurred. The military not only killed people, but sometimes tortured them in public and exposed their bodies. Citizens were forced to cooperate in these brutal counter-insurgency activities in the form of vigilante groups, with the structure of citizens killing citizens dividing society and causing trauma.[41] The United States provided technical support for these counter-insurgency

---

[38] Patrick Ball, Paul Kobrak, and Herbert F. Spirer, *State Violence in Guatemala, 1960–1996: A Quantitative Reflection* (Washington, D.C.: American Association for the Advancement of Science, 1999), Part II.

[39] The Commission for Historical Clarification (CEH), *Guatemala: Memory of Silence, Report of the Commission for Historical Clarification, Conclusions and Recommendations* (February 1999), para. 2.

[40] Ibid., para. 1.

[41] REMHI, eds., trans. Midori Iijima et al., *Guatemala, Never Again* [Japanese] (Tokyo: Iwanami Shoten, 2000), Part 1, Ch. 1.

activities and, through massive military aid, strengthened Guatemala's intelligence agencies and trained its officers.[42]

In the case of the Guatemalan Civil War, the government and the military were overwhelmingly stronger than the guerrillas. Therefore, through the conflict, all mass media were placed under the control of the government and the military, and the freedom to report on the massacres was almost eliminated. As a result, there were many cases where the fact of the massacre itself was buried in darkness. The dead cannot speak for themselves, and the only ones who could speak were the families and friends of those who were killed, or those who somehow survived the massacre. These survivors formed several human rights organizations to collect the facts of the massacres that were about to be buried from this world.

In 1993, some of these organizations came together to form the National Human Rights Coordinating Committee, and in 1996 they agreed to share information on disappearances and massacres, which was collected by the Centro Internacional para Investigaciones en Derechos. The data was sent to the Human Rights Data Analysis Group (HRDAG) and formed a comprehensive database. The person in charge of designing the database at HRDAG was Patrick Ball,[43] who later became a central figure in a network of experts who statistically analyze the number of conflict victims.

Towards the Generation of Statistical Data

In fact, this was not the first time that statistics and human rights issues were linked. In 1977, Carlos Noriega, an Argentine statistician and member of the American Statistical Association (ASA), was detained for refusing to falsify public statistical data at the request of the military regime, which became a major issue in the ASA. This led the ASA to actively discuss how statistics could address human rights violations, while calling for the release of scientists detained around the world,[44] with the results published as *Human Rights and Statistics* (1992).[45] The Guatemalan Civil War marked the first comprehensive application of statistics to war casualties.

How was the data on the number of victims of the Guatemalan Civil War created? To create statistical data, it is necessary to collect eyewitness testimonies from survivors. In Guatemala, several organizations, including HRDAG, independently dispatched research teams to various locations and conducted interviews with

---

42 Frederick H. Gareau, *State Terrorism and the United States: From Counterinsurgency to the War on Terrorism* (London: Zed Books, 2004), 61–63.

43 Patrick Ball and Megan Price, "The Statistics of Genocide," *Chance* 31, no. 1: 39. For Ball's career, see Tina Rosenberg, "The Body Counter: Meet Patrick Ball, A Statistician Who's Spent His Life Lifting the Fog of War," *Foreign Policy*, February 27, 2012.

44 Thomas B. Jabine and Douglas A. Samuelson, "Human Rights of Statisticians and Statistics of Human Rights: Early History of the American Statistical Association's Committee on Scientific Freedom and Human Rights," in *Statistical Methods for Human Rights*, ed. Jana Asher, David Banks, and Fritz J. Scheuren (New York; London: Springer, 2008).

45 T.B. Jabine and R.P. Claude, eds., *Human Rights and Statistics* (Philadelphia: University of Pennsylvania Press, 1992).

survivors. In quantitative social surveys, interviews are not based on individual questions, but on common questions; in other words, structured interviews are required.[46] The design of statistical data starts with creating the structure of these interviews. Facts are organized from the collected testimonies, but there are cases where multiple survivors testify about the same incident in different ways. The Guatemalan research organizations carefully classified these and summarized them one by one, turning them into data.

However, there was a serious limitation to the data generated in this way, that massacres that were not testified or reported were unintentionally excluded. In addition, in situations where the government and the military are overwhelmingly strong, it is easy to conceal massacres, which means that it becomes impossible to grasp the scale of the massacre. Therefore, a method was needed to count the dead that no one noticed. Patrick Ball asked for help from Fritz Scheuren, a statistician at the University of Chicago, who proposed a method called Multiple Systems Estimation (MSE), a calculation method that applies the mark-recapture method of animal population survey to humans. Here, without going into the details of the calculation method, I will only explain the general idea.

For example, suppose there are a certain number of fish in a pond and you want to know how many there are. In the mark-recapture method, you catch a number of fish, mark them, and return them to the pond. Then, you catch a number of fish in the pond again and count how many of the fish you caught are marked. You repeat this several times to collect data, and estimate the total number of fish based on this data. If there are few fish in the pond, the probability of recapturing a marked fish is high, and if there are many, it is low. Therefore, by repeating the capture, you can calculate the probability of capturing a marked fish and estimate the total number of fish from that probability.

How do we apply this to the number of deaths in conflict zones? Suppose several NGOs have independently created lists of conflict deaths in a certain conflict zone. The lists can be thought of as captures in the case of fish. If multiple lists have been created independently, they can be interpreted as repeated captures. There will be deaths reported to some NGOs, and there will also be deaths that are not reported for reasons such as having no relatives or all family members being dead. Or, there may be cases where the survey team could not find a witness by chance. Therefore, these lists are compared and the people who are duplicated between the lists are counted. These duplicates become the marked entities, so to speak, in the case of fish. Then, the total number is estimated based on these data. After that, calculate the bias of the list, derive the standard error, and the data is complete. This is the basic idea of MSE.[47]

---

[46] Ball and Price, "The Statistics of Genocide," 39.

[47] For a detailed explanation of the calculation method, see Patrick Ball, "The Guatemalan Commission for Historical Clarification: Generating Analytic Reports Inter-Sample Analysis," in *Making the Case: Investigating Large Scale Human Rights Violations Using Information Systems and Data Analysis*, ed. Patrick Ball, Herbert F. Spirer, and Louise Spirer (Washington: American Association for the Advancement of Science, 2000). For an overview and discussion of this method's issues, see Daniel Manrique-Vallier, Megan E. Price, and Anita Gohdes, "Multiple Systems Estimation

In the Guatemalan Civil War, in addition to the victim list of the CIIDH introduced earlier, there were lists from the Comisión para el Esclarecimiento Histórico (CEH) and the Recuperación de la Memoria Histórica (REMHI) of the Guatemalan Civil War, which were independently investigated and which made it possible to perform statistical analysis using MSE. The CEH is an organization established based on the Oslo Agreement signed by the Guatemalan government and the Guatemalan National Revolutionary Unity on June 23, 1994. The CEH aimed to clarify the facts about what kind of human rights violations were committed in the Guatemalan Civil War. However, as a result of political compromise, it was decided not to question the legal responsibility. The CEH conducted investigations with the support of the United Nations and published a 12-volume report in 1999.[48] In contrast, REMHI was a project initiated in 1995, spearheaded by the Catholic Church, to uncover the truth at the grassroots level. This project also conducted a large-scale investigation and published a four-volume report in 1998.[49]

Ball and his colleagues used data from CIIDH, CEH, and REMHI, and applied the MSE to estimate the total number of conflict victims. However, they conducted data analysis for a limited period from 1978 to 1996, not from 1960, and calculated the total number of victims to be 132,174 (standard error = 6568).[50] They concluded that 95.4% of the massacres were carried out by the state of Guatemala, and 4.6% were carried out by guerrillas.[51] Also, the total number of victims throughout the conflict period was estimated to be 20,000, which was recorded in the CEH report. However, this is not to say that there was no rebuttal. Carlos Sabino, an Argentine historian, re-examined the figures of CEH and REMHI, questioning whether many cases were duplicated and whether cases of deaths due to natural disasters were included. He argued that the actual number of deaths was far less than 20,000,[52] however, in subsequent studies of the Guatemalan civil war, the figure of 20,000 has not been overturned to date.

Techniques for Estimating Casualties in Armed Conflicts," in *Counting Civilian Casualties: An Introduction to Recording and Estimating Nonmilitary Deaths in Conflict*, ed. Taylor B. Seybolt, Jay D. Aronson, and Baruch Fischhoff (Oxford University Press, 2013); Nicholas P. Jewell, Michael Spagat, and Britta L. Jewell, "MSE and Casualty Counts: Assumptions, Interpretation, and Challenges," in *Counting Civilian Casualties: An Introduction to Recording and Estimating Nonmilitary Deaths in Conflict*, ed. Taylor B. Seybolt, Jay D. Aronson, and Baruch Fischhoff (Oxford University Press, 2013).

48 Christian Tomuschat, "Clarification Commission in Guatemala," *Human Rights Quarterly* 23, no. 2 (May 2001).

49 Kathy Ogle, "Guatemala's REMHI Project Memory from Below," *NACLA Report on the Americas* 32, no. 2: 33–34.

50 Ball, "The Guatemalan Commission for Historical Clarification," 270.

51 Ibid., 280.

52 Diane M. Nelson, *Who Counts? The Mathematics of Death and Life after Genocide* (Durham: Duke University Press, 2015), 63–64.

5.3 Discrepancy Between Statistical Surveys and Discourse

Estimation of the Number of Deaths in the Srebrenica Massacre

Just like the Guatemalan Civil War, the total number of conflict victims became a point of contention, and statistical analysis was conducted during the Yugoslav Wars of the 1990s. This conflict was a case where the movement for democratization in Yugoslavia at the end of the Cold War and the rise of nationalism in various regions collided, leading to a large-scale armed conflict. In this conflict, the International Criminal Tribunal for the former Yugoslavia (ICTY) was established, and conflict participants were held accountable for violations of international law, such as the massacre of civilians. The Yugoslav Wars are a collective term for several armed conflicts that occurred in this region, but here we will focus specifically on the armed conflict that occurred in Bosnia and Herzegovina (hereafter, the Bosnian War).

The ICTY Prosecutor's Office initiated a death toll research project related to the Bosnian War in 1997. The issue at hand was the Srebrenica massacre, a massacre that occurred in the town of Srebrenica in eastern Bosnia and Herzegovina in July 1995. Srebrenica was an area where mainly Muslim residents lived, surrounded by areas where many Serbian people lived. At one point, it became a base for attacking the residential areas of Serbian residents, but as Serbian forces became dominant, Srebrenica ultimately became the target of concentrated attacks. Srebrenica was designated as a safe zone by a UN Security Council resolution,[53] but the UN Protection Force (UNPROFOR) could not defend it, and the Muslim residents living there, as well as those who had flowed in from the surrounding areas, were unilaterally killed. When this incident was reported in the Western media, the impotence of the PKO and the brutality of the Serbian military forces became major international issues, and the momentum for intervention in the Bosnian War increased.

The Srebrenica massacre and the number of its victims became important points of contention at the ICTY. The experts in demography, including Norwegian demographer Helge Brunborg, were responsible for estimating the number of deaths in the Srebrenica massacre. Brunborg's research team used several data sets to estimate the number of deaths in Srebrenica. First, they used the missing and deceased lists, one created by the International Committee of the Red Cross (ICRC) and the other by the US-based international NGO Physicians for Human Rights (PHR). PHR is an organization formed mainly by American doctors who were dealing with human rights issues in Central and South America and elsewhere in 1986.

The ICRC conducted investigations into the missing persons in this conflict.[54] Under international humanitarian law, parties to a conflict have an obligation to provide information about the safety of those missing in relation to the conflict, which ICRC is permitted to investigate. During the investigation, the ICRC collected various information about the missing persons, not only their names and addresses but

[53] S/RES/819 (1993), April 16, 1993.

[54] ICMP, *Missing Persons from the Armed Conflicts of the 1990s: A Stocktaking on the Effort to Locate and Identify Missing Persons in Bosnia and Herzegovina* (Sarajevo: October 2014), 27–31.

also their clothing and physical characteristics, which made it possible to compare the information with that of the discovered bodies. In this way, a vast database based on personal information was created. Additionally, PHR conducted activities to investigate the identity and cause of death of bodies through forensic analysis (see Chap. 6); through these activities, they generated a database on missing persons and the deceased. The research team, in addition to these two types of data, used voter lists from elections held after the conflict to identify survivors, excluding them from the list of missing and deceased, with pre-war census records also used to verify whether the individuals truly existed. Following the MSE method, they counted the number of people commonly listed in these lists and estimated the number of deaths.[55]

Use of Evidence in Court

The research team's estimates were used as evidence in court in the first trial of Radislav Krstić. He was a commander of the Drina Corps, a Serbian military force belonging to the Army of Republika Srpska, accused of carrying out the massacre in Srebrenica. In June 2000, Brunborg testified in court about this estimate, reporting a calculation result that at least 7,475 people died in the Srebrenica massacre[56] (this number includes all deaths, including those from combat, disease, and suicide). In the trial in 2001, the ICTY considered this statistical data as one of the important pieces of evidence in estimating the number of people killed, along with survivor testimonies and forensic data.[57]

Even after 2000, the activities of the census team on the Bosnian War continued, and the death toll data was revised from time to time,[58] with DNA testing for identification playing a significant role in this revision process. The number of DNA tests was extremely large in proportion to the number of victims, and the International Commission on Missing Persons (ICMP) was responsible for this. The ICMP is an international organization established in Sarajevo with the aim of identifying missing persons in the former Yugoslav Wars, under the initiative of US President Bill Clinton at the G7 Summit in 1996.[59] The ICMP contracted with the PHR, which handled part of the forensic investigation work, and introduced DNA testing in full scale,

---

[55] Helge Brunborg, "Contribution of Statistical Analysis to the Investigations of the International Criminal Tribunals," *Statistical Journal of the United Nations Economic Commission for Europe* 18, no. 2–3 (2001): 227–38; Helge Brunborg, Torkild Hovde Lyngstad, and Henrik Urdal, "Accounting for Genocide: How Many Were Killed in Srebrenica?" *European Journal of Population* 19, no. 3 (2003): 229–48.

[56] Krstić Transcript, June 1, 2000, 4036–4067.

[57] Krstić Judgment, Trial Chamber, August 2, 2001, para. 81.

[58] Ewa Tabeau, *Conflict in Numbers: Casualties of the 1990s Wars in the Former Yugoslavia (1991–1999): Major Reports by Demographic Experts of the Prosecution in the Trials before the International Criminal Tribunal for the Former Yugoslavia* (Belgrade: Helsinki Committee for Human Rights in Serbia, 2009).

[59] For ICMP activities, see Ian Hanson, "Forensic Archaeology and the International Commission on Missing Persons: Setting Standards in an Integrated Process," in *Forensic Archaeology: A Global Perspective*, ed. W.J. Mike Groen, Nicholas Márquez-Grant, and Robert C. Janaway (Chichester, West Sussex: Wiley Blackwell, 2015); and ICMP, *Missing Persons*.

which greatly advanced the individual identification and identification of bodies. The activities of the ICMP will be discussed again in this chapter.[60]

The data on the number of victims, including the Srebrenica massacre, was also used in the trial of Radovan Karadžić. He was the first president of the Republika Srpska and the supreme commander of the Republika Srpska army, which is said to have carried out the massacre in Srebrenica. In the trial, Eva Tabeau, a Dutch demographer who was the leader of the census team of the ICTY Prosecutor's Office from 2000 to 2011, testified, presenting a demographic analysis of three cases, including Srebrenica. In their 2009 report, Tabeau and others stated that the number of victims in the Srebrenica massacre was 7,905 and, although the data has been updated from the report mentioned earlier by Brunborg, the number itself has not changed drastically. This figure was mentioned in the trial as reliable data for estimating the number of people killed.[61]

Scientific Numbers and Social Narratives

The ICTY has so far estimated the total number of deaths in the Bosnia-Herzegovina War, not just the Srebrenica massacre. In 2010, it expressed the view that about 10,000 people had died,[62] of which 40.2% were civilians and 59.8% were combatants,[63] and stated that the majority of the victims were Muslim residents. These figures are far removed from the previously widely circulated figure of 20,000. In the study of war casualties in the 1990s, which was mentioned in the introduction, 20,000 was considered the most reliable figure, but the more scientific figure was half of that. Also, thc proportion of civilians among the victims was not 80–90%.

Separate from the ICTY, in 2007, the NGO Research and Documentation Center based in Sarajevo announced preliminary survey results. The Research and Documentation Center was established in 2004 and received financial assistance from the Norwegian government. According to their survey results, about 97,000 people died in the war,[64] which roughly matches the ICTY's estimate and is still far from the 20,000. However, the results of the Research Record Center's investigation were met

---

[60] ICMP, *Missing Persons*, 52–53.

[61] Karadžić Judgment, Trial Chamber, March 24, 2016, para. 5572–578. In addition to the cases covered in this book, statistical data on war casualties by Patrick Ball was used in ICTY trials on the Kosovo conflict, providing crucial evidence to prove genocide. However, it should be noted that such statistical analysis alone cannot explain the cause of death. How did the 7,905 people in the Srebrenica incident lose their lives? According to a detailed analysis of the Srebrenica incident by Yukie Osa, approximately 5,000 people were executed, and the remaining 3,000 may have died in combat or from landmines. Yukie Osa, "Reconstructing the Srebrenica Incident: The Srebrenica Incident as an Established Fact and Prescription for Prevention of Recurrence" [Japanese], in *Srebrenica Genocide: Lessons and Challenges at the 25th Anniversary* (Tokyo: Tohshindo, 2020) [Japanese], 31.

[62] Jan Zwierzchowski and Ewa Tabeau, "The 1992–95 War in Bosnia and Herzegovina: Census-Based Multiple System Estimation of Casualties' Undercount," Paper for International Research Workshop on "The Global Economic Costs of Conflict," Berlin, February 2010, 15.

[63] Ibid., 15–16.

[64] Lara J. Nettelfield, "Research and Repercussions of Death Tolls: The Case of the Bosnian Book of the Dead," in *Sex, Drugs, and Body Counts: The Politics of Numbers in Global Crime and Conflict*,

with fierce backlash and criticism from the local community. The Bosnian government claimed that there were more than 20,000 victims, while Serbian politicians protested that the proportion of Serbian victims was too low. Prominent researchers at local universities also claimed that the center's investigation was unfair, and even went as far as to personally attack the person responsible for the investigation and criticize the Norwegian government. Despite the scientific validity of the NGO's investigation results being confirmed after checks by experts in war population theory such as Tabeau, the backlash against the numbers did not subside.[65]

However, this debate was only conducted in the local media and did not fundamentally overturn the results of scientific analyses, including the ICTY's investigation. As can be seen from this issue, even data with high scientific durability does not necessarily gain social trust, with the calculation of statistical data too complex and difficult for many citizens. Moreover, each community has its own narrative about the war, and data that conflicts with this is not easily accepted.

5.4 Wars Without Neutral Numbers

Fact-Finding by the United Nations

The Syrian conflict was another case where it was difficult to grasp the number of victims, in a different way from the former Yugoslav Wars. In March 2011, peaceful protests against the Assad regime broke out in major Syrian cities, but security forces killed dozens of citizens in an attempt to suppress the spread of the movement. Despite this, the protest movement expanded further, eventually escalating into armed conflict between the regime and the opposition. Data on the humanitarian situation and the number of victims of the Syrian conflict have been collected and reported mainly by the UN Human Rights Council and the Office of the High Commissioner for Human Rights (OHCHR). However, the method of how the number of victims has been investigated requires focus.

At the end of April 2011, in view of the deteriorating situation in Syria, the UN Human Rights Council requested the OHCHR to investigate the humanitarian situation. In June, the OHCHR conducted investigations, such as interviews with people who had fled from Syria, and published a report three months later which concluded that the Syrian government was not fulfilling its responsibility to protect its citizens from crimes against humanity.[66] During the same period, the Human Rights Council established an independent international commission chaired by Paulo Pinheiro, which began a full-scale investigation into the human rights situation in Syria. The

---

ed. Peter Andreas and Kelly M. Greenhill (Ithaca and London: Cornell University Press, 2010), 162–65.

[65] Nettelfield, "Research and Repercussions of Death Tolls," 166–73; Patrick Ball, Ewa Tabeau, and Philip Verwimp, "The Bosnian Book of Dead: Assessment of the Database (Full Report)," HiCN Research Design Notes 5 (June 17, 2007).

[66] A/HRC/18/53, September 15, 2011.

commission was unable to obtain the cooperation of the Syrian government and could not conduct investigations on the ground. Nevertheless, they made efforts to collect primary data, such as conducting interviews with more than 200 related parties. As a result, it was found that by early November 2011, 3,500 civilians had already been killed by the Syrian army.[67] They also revealed that various human rights abuses, including the use of excessive violence and extrajudicial executions, were being carried out by the Syrian government,[68] however, the independent international commission did not consider the situation in Syria to be subject to international humanitarian law. At the time of the investigation, they concluded that the military conflict in Syria had not escalated to the level of internal armed conflict envisaged by humanitarian law.[69]

Civil wars, unlike wars between nations, do not necessarily become intense combat from the beginning. Initially, there is often government repression and small-scale resistance movements against it, which is not yet a war; this gradually escalates and develops into intense armed conflict, only becoming recognized as a category of war when the exchange of violence exceeds a certain level. The problem is this standard of judging. The independent international commission, in its investigation report, referred to the case law of the ICTY and cited the intensity of the armed conflict and the degree of organization of the conflict actors as criteria for determining whether it was a war.[70] "Intensity of conflict" refers to the level of violence, but what does "degree of organization" mean? For example, consider a region with poor security. There, murders occur every day, and the number of deaths due to murder is higher than the number of deaths due to heart disease. Now, is this a civil war? No, it is not; it is just poor security. War is a phenomenon where organized violence clashes, not a collection of individual murder cases. In a war, a command and control system is established among the belligerents, and a large number of murders are planned accordingly. Therefore, the "degree of organization of conflict actors" is included in the requirements for war.

As of November 2011, the Free Syrian Army (FSA) and the Syrian National Council (SNC), which would become the central forces of the opposition, had just been established and were hardly in a state of being fully organized. Both organizations were unable to establish legitimacy within Syria and lacked the ability to control the anti-government movement.[71] The independent commission judged that this was not yet a war.

However, after this, the situation in Syria deteriorated further, taking on the appearance of a full-scale civil war. In December 2011, UN High Commissioner for Human

---

[67] A/HRC/S-17/2/Add.1, November 23, 2011, para. 28.

[68] Ibid., para. 84–96.

[69] Ibid., para. 97.

[70] Ibid., para. 98.

[71] Motomichi Igarashi, "U.S. Reluctant Interventions and Sovereignty: The Cases of Libya and Syria" [Japanese], *Political Science Year Book*, II (2019), 85–86.

Rights Navi Pillay described the crisis in Syria as a civil war.[72] The next day, the UN Human Rights Council strongly condemned human rights abuses by the Syrian government through a resolution.[73] In January of the following year, the Syrian government claimed that the condemnation of human rights abuses was mistaken and that all responsibility lay with armed terrorist groups.[74] In February, intense fighting broke out over Homs, Syria's third-largest city and referred to as the "center of the revolution," which was reportedly subjected to a large-scale attack by the Assad regime.[75] Under these circumstances, the UN and the Arab League appointed former UN Secretary-General Kofi Annan as a joint special envoy and dispatched him to Syria. After negotiations, on April 12, the Syrian government and the opposition agreed to a ceasefire, and the United Nations Supervision Mission in Syria (UNSMIS) began operations in Syria. However, the ceasefire collapsed after about two weeks, and UNSMIS was unable to continue its activities, ending its organizational activities in August. In August 2012, the independent international commission released its third report on Syria which recognized for the first time that the situation in Syria was an internal armed conflict as envisaged by humanitarian law.[76] Although it did not detail what specific data this judgment was based on, it pointed out that the organization of the opposition had progressed.[77]

Another important point of discussion was the number of conflict-related deaths, which was a crucial data point when considering the scale of the armed conflict. As of July 2012, several non-governmental organizations and anti-government forces in Syria announced that the death toll had reached between 17,000 and 22,000. However, in contrast to these data, the Syrian government claimed it was around 7,928. Although there was a significant discrepancy in the numbers, the report of the commission was unable to clarify which was closer to the actual situation, and merely listed these figures.[78] From this, we can see the difficulty in estimating the number of casualties in the Syrian conflict. The biggest problem with the Syrian conflict is that neither the data from the Assad regime, the anti-government forces, nor the local NGOs can be considered neutral. Moreover, it is not easy for UN staff or international NGO personnel to enter the conflict zone and conduct their own investigations; in fact, the UN announced in January 2014 that it would stop counting the number of deaths in the Syrian conflict. In the case of the Syrian conflict, unlike the Guatemalan Civil War or the former Yugoslav Wars, it was necessary to estimate the number of casualties in an ongoing war. Therefore, data collection was the biggest issue.

---

[72] United Nations, "Syrian Crisis Reaching Stage of Civil War, UN Human Rights Chief Says," *UN News*, December 1, 2011.

[73] A/HRC/RES/S-18/1, December 2, 2012.

[74] Alan Cowell and Steven Lee Myers, "U.N. Panel Accuses Syrian Government of Crimes Against Humanity," *New York Times*, February 23, 2012.

[75] Christopher Phillips, *The Battle for Syria: International Rivalry in the New Middle East* (New Haven: Yale University Press, 2016), 86.

[76] A/HRC/RES/S-18/1, December 2, 2012, Annex II Applicable Law.

[77] Ibid., Annex III Military Situation.

[78] A/HRC/21/50, August 16, 2012, para. 38–39.

Estimating the Number of Casualties

To address the difficult task of estimating the number of casualties, OHCHR sought the cooperation of the Human Rights Data Analysis Group at the non-profit organization Benetech. Benetech, an organization that has been conducting humanitarian activities based on IT technology with the support of Microsoft, was part of this investigation.[79] The research group included Patrick Ball, who had become an authority on war statistics since his investigation in Guatemala.

What the Benetech research group focused on was data on casualties. In Syria, there were various organizations with different political positions, each recording casualties, and, therefore, the research group selected the following seven records from the many available and decided to analyze them: (1) the Violations Documentation Centre; (2) the Syrian Network for Human Rights; (3) the Syrian Revolution General Council; (4) the Syria Shuhada Website; (5) the March 15 Group; (6) the Syrian Observatory for Human Rights; and (7) the Syrian government. After examining each record in detail, it was found that the data from the Syrian Network for Human Rights was derived from the data of the Syrian Revolution General Council, and the two were treated as one data set; as a result, they were organized as six data sets.[80] From each of the six data sets, only those that could identify the victim's name, date of death, and location were extracted, and a comparison was made using the six data sets. Naturally, it is conceivable that the same case is recorded by multiple organizations, so any duplicates had to be subtracted. The research group collected possible matching combinations, created a single data set, and, from this, made match/non-match judgments, creating training data for AI to generate match/non-match algorithms. Then, based on this training data, AI automatically judged the match/non-match of all data.[81]

The use of such AI is double-edged. On the positive side, tasks that were previously done manually can now be automated by AI, potentially saving labor and time. On the negative side, if the use of AI progresses too far, it may become a black box, and there may be a risk of not being able to bear the responsibility of explanation. The algorithms that AI generates from training data are not necessarily the same as the rules in human minds. In 2016, AlphaGo, developed by DeepMind, defeated a world-class Go player, with AlphaGo learning 30 million moves from top players and strengthening itself by repeatedly playing games. Currently, AI is generating its own algorithms in various fields, including image recognition, by repeating analysis and learning. However, AI states conclusions but does not explain the contents of its algorithms. Even if the conclusion is correct, part of the process remains unknown. Also, if there are biases or mistakes in the training data itself, the algorithm may

---

[79] https://www.microsoft.com/en-us/ai/ai-for-humanitarian-action-projects?activetab=pivot1:primaryr7.

[80] Megan Price, Jeff Klingner, and Patrick Ball, "Preliminary Statistical Analysis of Documentation of Killings in the Syrian Arab Republic" (January 2, 2013), 2–3.

[81] *Ibid.*, 29–31.

continue to reproduce these biases or mistakes.[82] However, while these problems are pointed out, the application range of AI is rapidly expanding. The field of DAC is also part of this.

Returning to the topic, from this data, with duplicates removed, the research group derived the number of victims as 59,698 (limited to the period from March 2011 to November 2012). OHCHR and Benetech conducted similar surveys several times afterwards, and found 92,901 people from March 2011 to April 2013,[83] and 191,369 people from March 2011 to April 2014.[84] As the research group has cautioned, these figures may include overlooked duplicates, while cases of death not included in any organization's records are not included in the calculation; therefore, the number could be significantly underestimated. However, they did not estimate statistical data including unreported deaths from these data, which is a major difference from the Guatemalan Civil War and the former Yugoslav Wars. Nevertheless, the significance of producing as accurate a number as possible with the available data is by no means small.

The Syrian conflict then continued, with the total number of victims of the entire conflict remaining unclear. Organizations such as the Syrian Human Rights Observatory regularly announced the total number of victims, but such organizations were not neutral and there was criticism that the numbers were biased.[85] Indeed, the criticism is valid, but in the Syrian conflict, there probably was no organization that was politically neutral and was collecting DAC rooted in the local area.

Under such circumstances, in June 2022, OHCHR published a report on the Syrian conflict, concluding that 306,887 civilians died in the conflict over the ten years from March 2011 to March 2021.[86] However, this number is not the total number of conflict victims, but the number of civilian deaths only. OHCHR used eight types of data collected by Syrian NGOs, etc., to derive this data. From there, duplicates were identified and subtracted, resulting in a recorded death toll of 352,209 (of which 143,350 were civilians). OHCHR then used the Multiple System Estimation (MSE) to estimate the number of unrecorded civilian deaths as 163,537, added it to the aforementioned total of 143,350, and derived the total number of civilian deaths (306,887).[87] They then further derived the standard error of the data and estimated that the actual number was between 281,443 and 337,971. However, this is only the number of civilian deaths, and if the number of combatant casualties is included, it will be much higher. This data generated by OHCHR was the result of statistical

[82] Hannah Fry, *Hello World: How to Be Human in the Age of the Machine* (London: Doubleday, 2018).

[83] Megan Price, Jeff Klingner, and Patrick Ball, "Updated Statistical Analysis of Documentation of Killings in the Syrian Arab Republic," June 13, 2013.

[84] Megan Price, Anita Gohdes, and Patrick Ball, "Updated Statistical Analysis of Documentation of Killings in the Syrian Arab Republic," August 2014.

[85] For example, Hiroyuki Aoyama, "The Bias Hidden in Victim Statistics of the Syrian Observatory for Human Rights and the Syrian Network for Human Rights" [Japanese], https://news.yahoo.co.jp/byline/aoyamahiroyuki/20151220-00052626.

[86] A/HRC/50/68, June 28, 2022.

[87] Ibid., para. 23–24.

know-how on war damage accumulated from the Guatemalan Civil War.

*

In this chapter, we have looked at the activities of statistical analysis for measuring the dead in war. Since the eighteenth century, nations have used statistics to understand society. War was one of the areas where such statistics were used, however, statistical data in war is very difficult to guarantee accuracy. As the case of the Vietnam War revealed, there is a strong incentive for the military to falsify when collecting statistical data. Especially in an authoritarian regime, it is impossible to expect accuracy in data on human rights abuses and violations of humanitarian law. Therefore, statistical surveys by humanitarian networks were important.

In Guatemala, statistical analysis was conducted in the process of investigations such as the Truth Commission, and the total number of conflict victims was estimated. In the former Yugoslav Wars, such statistical data was used not only to clarify the reality, but also in international criminal trials, contributing to the pursuit of legal responsibility. Furthermore, in the Syrian conflict, the United Nations was able to produce data with some scientific durability in a situation where local investigations were extremely difficult. Humanitarian networks have grown and made technical progress with each conflict investigation.

However, as the case of the Bosnian War revealed, even if scientific durability increases, social credibility does not necessarily follow suit. The figures for the number of conflict deaths are important not only for understanding the scale of damage, but also for creating social narratives. Therefore, in situations like the Syrian conflict, where it is difficult to have a neutral position, it is even more difficult to determine the number of victims. Moreover, statistical calculations often require specialized knowledge and are difficult for many citizens. Even though a certain number is determined, whether it is politically and socially accepted is a separate issue from scientific accuracy.

Chapter 6
Unearthing the Bodies: War and Forensic Science

Contents

Abstract This chapter examines the role of forensic science in the generation of DAC. Forensic experts play a pivotal role in investigating the manner of death of each individual who perished in war. Forensic science, which has rapidly developed since World War II, has been applied to the analysis of war casualties and has gradually begun to generate accurate data. In Argentina during the late 1970s, a civilian group was established to search for missing persons, which subsequently led to the formation of a network of forensic experts. This network subsequently played an active role in the Yugoslav Wars. The network of forensic experts formed in this way was a global one, connecting professional institutions around the world. This network played a significant role in the establishment of the ICTY and in the trials. The data generated by this network of forensic experts was instrumental in questioning the legal responsibility of those who violated international law.

Even though we can statistically grasp the damage of war, it does not explain how each individual lost their life. If we aspire to truly comprehend the nature of war, it is imperative that we investigate in detail who these victims were and how they died. Especially if the legal responsibility for their death is to be questioned in court, it is necessary to clarify who was killed and how, which is where forensic science comes in. Forensic science is a field that applies various scientific expertise in the analysis of human remains and related objects based on the context of law.[1] This field is

[1] For forensic science, see, for example, Roxana Ferllini, ed., *Forensic Archaeology and Human Rights Violations* (Springfield: Charles C. Thomas, 2007); W.J. Mike Groen, Nicholas Márquez-Grant, and Robert C. Janaway, eds., *Forensic Archaeology: A Global Perspective* (Chichester, West Sussex: Wiley Blackwell, 2015); Soren Blau and Douglas H. Ubelaker, eds., *Handbook of Forensic Anthropology and Archaeology* (London: Routledge, 2016).

M. Igarashi, *War and Data on Armed Conflicts*, Evidence-Based Approaches to Peace and Conflict Studies 14, https://doi.org/10.1007/978-981-97-6418-1_6

composed of forensic anthropology, forensic archaeology, forensic pathology, etc., and has played an important role in investigating the reality of conflicts. The previous chapter focused on statistical analysis that captures war on a macro scale, but this chapter focuses on forensic analysis that captures war on a micro scale.

Specifically, this book clarifies the role that forensic science has played in the generation of DAC, focusing on the case of the International Criminal Tribunal for the former Yugoslavia (ICTY). As previously mentioned, the ICTY is an international criminal court established by the United Nations Security Council in 1993. Its purpose was to prosecute those who committed mass killings, war crimes, and crimes against humanity in the former Yugoslavia, and it completed all trials and closed in 2017.

6.1 Role of Forensic Investigations

Accumulation of Forensic Research

Since the mid-nineteenth century, nations have taken on the responsibility of collecting information about the deaths of soldiers and explaining it to their families. This necessitated the investigation of the identities of the remaining bodies, with the invention of the dog tag, as mentioned in Chap. 2, making this identification easier. In identification, a soldier's belongings are an important clue. In addition, there are cases where the identity is inferred from characteristics such as the skeleton and teeth.[2] During World War I, forensic anthropology was not so developed, and the belongings left behind, centered on dog tags, were the biggest clue to identification.[3]

Forensic anthropology emerged as a full-fledged academic field when Wilton Marion Krogman published a paper in the United States in 1939 called "A Guide to the Identification of Human Skeletal Material."[4] Since then, in the field of forensic anthropology, a body of knowledge that scientifically derives characteristics such as sex and age from the analysis of human bones has been generated. In fact, it is a very difficult and specialized task to take out a part of a human bone and determine which part it is. Moreover, identifying the person from there requires a lot of research accumulation.

In wars, a large number of unidentified bodies are left behind, and forensic anthropologists are essential for their investigation. Japan has been conducting forensic investigations of war dead overseas since 1950, and in recent years, projects for the collection of remains, including forensic investigations, have been intermittently carried out in the islands of the Pacific and Sakhalin.[5] Characteristics such as age at

[2] For details on the identification of war dead, see Hanihara Kazuro, *Bones Speak of Humans* (Tokyo: Kodansha, 1997) [Japanese].

[3] Victoria Martin, "A First World War Example of Forensic Archaeology," *Forensic Science International* 314 (2020): 3.

[4] Clyde Collins Snow, "Forensic Anthropology," *Annual Review of Anthropology* 11 (1982).

[5] Shuichiro Narasaki, *Final Testimony of Soldiers through Bones: The Truth of Pacific War and the Collection of War Dead Remains* (Tokyo: Chikuma Shobo, 2018) [Japanese].

death, gender, and ethnicity can be determined from skeletal and dental features, and affiliations can be inferred from clothing and personal belongings. This is not limited to Japan, and is carried out in many countries that participated in World War II. In the case of the United States, even after World War II, there were many casualties in the Korean War and the Vietnam War, and the method of identification developed significantly. The bodies of American soldiers from the Korean War were identified at the US military base in Kokura (Japan), with Japanese university officials also participating.[6]

If a state investigates the bodies of its soldiers who died in battle, those soldiers are still fortunate. In the case of unilateral massacres or civil wars by authoritarian regimes, it is rare for the state to take responsibility for collecting forensic data of those killed. In such cases, citizens turn to international humanitarian networks for help, with NGOs and international organizations possibly forming investigation teams to collect forensic data and dispatch them to areas where massacres or civil wars have occurred. For example, as will be discussed later, families and friends of missing persons may request such humanitarian networks to investigate in order to find out about their whereabouts. Alternatively, when the international community raises the issue of massacre and the International Criminal Court initiates an investigation, forensic investigations are conducted by humanitarian networks.

International Criminal Trials and Forensic Science

Just like in domestic criminal trials, in international criminal trials, explaining the attributes and cause of death of the deceased is extremely important in proving a crime, which is where analysis of the body is needed. The investigation typically begins with the discovery of mass graves where bodies are buried. In the event of a massacre during a war, it is more common to bury bodies together in one place rather than individually. Once the burial site is found, bodies are exhumed from there. The attributes and cause of death should be revealed by comprehensively analyzing the circumstances of discovery, relics, physical characteristics, and damage conditions of the body. Forensic experts, such as forensic archaeologists, forensic anthropologists, and forensic pathologists, are involved in this data generation process.

However, the death data generated here is interpreted only within the scope of expert knowledge. For example, forensic scientists present a bundle of possibilities for the cause of death, but do not select one of them or add a legal interpretation to it. They do not discuss the attribution of the crime, which is particularly problematic. In other words, even though forensic scientists examine the body, they do not, in principle, infer who committed what crime. Legal judgments and the determination of forensic facts are delineated.

Furthermore, forensic investigations are conducted to reveal that a certain pattern existed in the crime, and are not necessarily intended to reveal the full picture of the conflict. In criminal trials, it is sufficient to extract the information necessary to prove

[6] Michael Sledge, *Soldier Dead: How We Recover, Identify, Bury, and Honor Our Military Fallen* (New York: Columbia University Press, 2005). For details on the body investigation in Kokura, see Hanihara, *Bones Speak of Humans*.

the crime, and it is not necessary to clarify where and how the crime was committed in every detail. In the case of mass murder, if we wait for such clarification, the trial will never end. Thus, comprehensive investigations into the conflict and forensic investigations related to the trial are distinguished in principle.

A certain degree of objectivity and independence is required of the forensic investigation team. The ICTY was composed of the Chambers, the Registry and the Office of the Prosecutor (OTP), while the forensic investigation team belonged to the OTP in terms of organizational structure. However, the forensic investigation team had a system in place to avoid providing as much contextual and background knowledge as possible at the analysis stage, which was to prevent any bias from occurring in the analysis. In fact, the presence or absence of bias in the analyst was disputed in the ICTY trials, with the judgment holding that even though limited background knowledge is given to forensic experts, it cannot be said to cast doubt on the credibility of the report.[7] The forensic investigation team, at least in principle, worked not for the OTP but to present objective facts necessary for the trial, and its principles of action were based on scientific requirements in forensics.

In international criminal trials, only the necessary data is selected and used from various data to prove the crime. The data on the deceased required in international criminal trials is mainly the cause of death and general attributes. Therefore, it does not necessarily satisfy the remaining family members. Many families strongly desire identification of the deceased, and want to know the details of how their loved ones met their end, however, it is not always necessary to clarify this in proving a crime in court.[8] Therefore, humanitarian networks that generate DAC are often asked to generate different types of deceased data for families, separate from the trial.[9] In this way, DAC needs to be adjusted according to its purpose and required function.

6.2 Establishment of the International Criminal Tribunal for the Former Yugoslavia

The Journey to the Establishment of the ICTY

We will now examine the role of forensics in trials at the ICTY. Forensic investigations were deeply involved in the establishment of the ICTY itself. In April 1992, when

---

[7] ICTY, Prosecutor v. Karadžić (Case IT-95-5/18-T), Judgment, Trial Chamber, March 24, 2016, para. 5530.

[8] Eric Stover and Rachel Shigekane, "The Missing in the Aftermath of War: When Do the Needs of Victims' Families and International War Crimes Tribunals Clash?" *International Review of the Red Cross* 84 (2002): 846, 848. Of course, the desires of families vary, and they cannot be treated uniformly.

[9] In the case of Rwanda, identification was not often conducted due to opposition from the Rwandan government and others to forensic identification. Remi Korman, "Bury or Display? The Politics of Exhumation in Post-Genocide Rwanda," in *Human Remain and Identification: Mass Violence, Genocide, and the 'Forensic Turn'*, ed. Elisabeth Anstett and Jean-Marc Dreyfus (Manchester University Press, 2015).

a full-scale armed conflict broke out in Bosnia, the United Nations Commission on Human Rights (CHR) appointed a special rapporteur about four months later to investigate the human rights situation in the region. The special rapporteur at this time was Tadeusz Mazowiecki, a former Prime Minister of Poland who was known as a leader who promoted the democratization movement. The first on-site investigation was conducted from August 21 to 26, 1992, and the first report was submitted on August 28.

In this investigation, Mazowiecki sought the cooperation of Louis Joinet, the chairman of the United Nations Arbitrary Detention Working Group, and Bacre W. Ndiaye, the United Nations Special Rapporteur on Extrajudicial, Summary or Arbitrary Executions.[10] They conducted interviews with many stakeholders through on-site investigations and other means. Because it was a conflict zone, the places they could visit were limited,[11] and they even encountered interference from Serbian forces,[12] making the investigation difficult. However, they eventually collected many testimonies and concluded that ethnic cleansing, as well as unjust detention, execution, and forced disappearances, had taken place.[13]

The second on-site investigation was conducted in October 1992, and the investigation staff was increased at this time. Among them were two forensic scientists, including Clyde Snow.[14] The forensic experts were mainly tasked with identifying the locations where bodies related to the incident were buried and analyzing the characteristics of the bodies. In fact, one of the mass burial sites that led to the most important evidence of war crimes was discovered in this investigation,[15] laying the groundwork necessary for collecting physical evidence of war crimes.

Concurrently with the CHR, the Secretary-General of the United Nations established an expert committee to investigate serious violations of humanitarian law in the conflict, based on the request of the Security Council.[16] This committee was composed of five experts in humanitarian law and was chaired by Frits Kalshoven, an international affairs advisor to the Netherlands Red Cross and a member of the International Fact-Finding Commission.[17] This expert committee took on the comprehensive coordination of various actors conducting investigations into violations of humanitarian law, including the CHR.

---

[10] E/CN.4/1992/S-1/9, August 28, 1992, para. 3.

[11] Ibid., para. 5.

[12] Tadeusz Mazowiecki, "Will to Disaster," *Index on Censorship* 24, no. 5 (September 1995): 70.

[13] E/CN.4/1992/S-1/9, August 28, 1992.

[14] E/CN.4/1992/S-1/10, October 27, 1992, para. 2–3.

[15] Ibid., para. 18 and Annex II.

[16] Alfred de Zayas, "The Kalshoven Commission," *Leiden Journal of International Law* 6, no. 1 (April 1993): 131.

[17] The International Fact-Finding Commission is an organization established under Article 90 of the Additional Protocol I to the Geneva Conventions of 1977 to investigate violations of humanitarian law. This organization has yet to operate in an actual armed conflict.

Western countries had begun to consider the possibility of criminal trials in addition to investigations into war crimes at this stage.[18] In November, the expert committee and the Conference on Security and Cooperation in Europe (CSCE) agreed to conduct investigations into legal responsibility and activities towards the establishment of an International Criminal Court.[19] The following month, the CSCE formally decided to draft a treaty on the establishment of the International Criminal Court.[20]

Dispatch of Forensic Experts

From December 15 to 20, a preliminary investigation was finally conducted to collect physical evidence of war crimes.[21] The United Nations' Special Rapporteur on Extra-judicial, Summary or Arbitrary Executions, Ndiaye, took charge and dispatched an investigation team. The team, led by Canadian military legal officer William J. Fenrick, conducted a preliminary forensic investigation at suspected massacre sites.[22] This investigation required forensic experts, so they sought support from the international NGO Physicians for Human Rights (PHR), based in the United States. At that time, there was already a network in the United States, centered around PHR, that specialized in forensic investigations of conflicts and human rights abuses. The key figures were Eric Stover, then executive director of PHR, and forensic authority Clyde Snow. Despite the extremely dangerous environment due to the ongoing conflict, they investigated four suspected mass burial sites and revealed the potential existence of evidence of war crimes.

The relationship between Stover and Snow can be traced back to the investigation of the disappeared during Argentina's Dirty War (1976–1983).[23] At that time, under the military dictatorship in Argentina, a large number of ordinary citizens had disappeared, and there were many reports of mothers and children being kidnapped and remaining missing. In order to investigate the identities of their kidnapped grandchildren, the Grandmothers of the Plaza de Mayo was formed. However, there were no forensic experts in Argentina under the dictatorship who could meet their needs, so they sought support from the American Association for the Advancement of Science (AAAS).[24] Stover was a staff member of the AAAS at the time, and Snow was part of the support group which he created.[25] Snow was already active as a forensic expert in the United States, and asked for investigative cooperation from the experts

---

[18] William A. Schabas, *The UN International Criminal Tribunals: The Former Yugoslavia, Rwanda and Sierra Leone* (Cambridge: Cambridge University Press, 2006), 14–16.

[19] S/25274, February 10, 1993, Annex I, para. 19.

[20] "Rapporteurs' Mission under the CSCE Moscow Human Dimension Mechanism to Bosnia-Herzegovina and Croatia," in ICTY, *Path to the Hague, The Selected Documents on the Origins of the ICTY* (Hague: International Criminal Tribunal for the former Yugoslavia, 2001), 79–81.

[21] E/CN.4/1993/50, February 10, 1993, Annex I.

[22] John Hagan, *Justice in the Balkans: Prosecuting War Crimes in the Hague Tribunal* (Chicago and London: The University of Chicago Press, 2003), 39–40.

[23] Eric Stover and Gilles Peress, *The Graves: Srebrenica and Vukovar* (Zürich: Scalo, 1998), 109.

[24] Eric Stover and Molly Ryan, "Breaking Bread with the Dead," *Historical Archaeology* 35, no. 1 (2001): 9.

[25] Bradley Graham, "On the Track of Killings in Argentina," *The Washington Post*, June 23, 1987.

of Argentine universities but was refused, so he educated local university students to be his staff.[26] This led to the establishment of the NGO the Argentine Forensic Anthropology Team, which analyzed the bodies of people who were likely to have disappeared under the military regime. The students educated here became forensic experts and later participated in forensic investigations in the former Yugoslavia.[27]

Investigation of Mass Burial Sites

In 1992, a forensic investigation team, including Snow, conducted an investigation of mass burial sites, primarily in Vukovar (a town currently located in the eastern part of Croatia). They discovered one of the mass burial sites in a rural area. However, they did not receive sufficient cooperation from local Serbian military officials or peacekeeping personnel, making the investigation difficult.[28] Nevertheless, they discovered some evidence of the massacre within the deadline. According to a report issued in January 1993, it was estimated that about 200 bodies were buried in that burial site. As a result of the analysis, it was concluded that the people who were killed were executed on the spot. When matched with witness information, it was believed that the bodies were wounded soldiers, civilians, and staff from local hospitals. Also, from the remaining items, it was clear that those buried there were Croatian residents.[29]

In February 1993, based on these reports of war crimes, a committee of experts chaired by Kalshoven proposed the establishment of an International Criminal Tribunal to judge war crimes in the former Yugoslav Wars.[30] About three months later, the establishment of the International Criminal Tribunal was recommended by the UN Secretary-General, and the adoption of Security Council Resolution 827, which formally decided the establishment, was realized.[31]

6.3 Investigation of the Srebrenica Massacre

Start of the Investigation

Forensic investigations played a crucial role not only in the establishment of the ICTY but also in actual trials. One of the cases that well illustrates this is the investigation into the Srebrenica massacre. As explained earlier, this incident was a massacre that occurred in July 1995. Srebrenica was an area mainly inhabited by Muslim residents,

---

[26] Luis Fondebrider and Vivian Scheinsohn, "Forensic Archaeology: the Argentinian Way," in *Forensic Archaeology: A Global Perspective*, ed. W. J. Mike Groen, Nicholas Márquez-Grant, and Robert C. Janaway (Chichester, West Sussex: Wiley Blackwell, 2015).

[27] Howard Ball, *Working in the Killing Fields: Forensic Science in Bosnia* (Washington, D.C.: Potomac Books, 2015), Ch. 3; Fondebrider and Scheinsohn, "Forensic Archaeology".

[28] Stover and Peress, *The Graves*, 111–12.

[29] S/25274, February 10, 1993, Annex II Report of a Preliminary Site Exploration of a Mass Grave near Vukovar, Former Yugoslavia.

[30] Ibid., Annex I, para. 74.

[31] S/RES/827, May 25, 1993.

surrounded by areas where many Serbs lived. When the Serb forces became dominant in the conflict, Srebrenica eventually became the target of concentrated attacks, and a large number of Muslim residents and prisoners living there (and those who had flowed in from the surrounding areas) were killed.

The full-scale body investigation of the Srebrenica massacre began around April 1996 and continued until 2001 (preliminary investigations started from July 1995). In cases of war and mass murder, it is not uncommon for a long time to pass before the issue comes to light and on-site investigations are conducted. This incident was somewhat unique in that a forensic investigation was conducted immediately after the massacre, securing a lot of evidence. The chief investigator was Jean-René Ruez, a former French police officer,[32] and his team discovered more than 40 burial sites and exhumed bodies from about half of them.[33] As mentioned earlier, forensic investigations begin by identifying the location of the burial site. Aerial photos provided by the CIA and testimonies from those involved in the Srebrenica massacre, as well as survivors who escaped from the scene, played a crucial role in this work.[34] The investigation team matched these, and discovered the burial sites while moving back and forth from the scene.

Afterwards, the excavation of the bodies began, but the situation was somewhat complicated in the case of Srebrenica. This was because the Serbian military forces, fearing the exposure of the massacre, dug up the burial sites and reburied some of the bodies in different locations (known as secondary burial sites).[35] In the process, many bodies were severely damaged, or a single body was destroyed and buried in various places. When a body is damaged, naturally, it becomes difficult to identify the person or analyze the cause of death.

The forensic analysis of bodies in mass murders proceeded roughly as follows. First, the excavation of the burial sites was carried out based on the knowledge of forensic archaeology, which specializes in the excavation of bodies. The excavation investigation in Srebrenica in 1996 was led by William Haglund, an American forensic anthropologist.[36] In conflict zones, burial sites cannot be excavated immediately. Often, they are in minefields, so mine detection is necessary before excavation. However, the investigation team initially could not get the cooperation of the United

---

32 Hagan, *Justice in the Balkans*, 132–33. Also, for Jean-René Ruez, see Hiroto Fujiwara, "International Criminal Investigation by ICTY and Srebrenica" [Japanese], in *Srebrenica Genocide: Lessons and Challenges on its 25th Anniversary* (Tokyo: Toshindo, 2020), 107–49.

33 Karadžić Judgment, Trial Chamber, March 24, 2016, para. 5523.

34 Hagan, *Justice in the Balkans*, 137–41.

35 Admir Jugo and Sari Wastell, "Disassembling the Pieces, Reassembling the Social: The Forensic and Political Lives of Secondary Mass Graves in Bosnia and Herzegovina," in *Human Remain and Identification: Mass Violence, Genocide, and the 'Forensic Turn'* (Manchester: Manchester University Press, 2015), 150–51. For the geographical relationship between primary and secondary burial sites, see ICMP, *Missing Persons*, 97.

36 Jean-René Ruez, "Les enquêtes du TPIY. Entretien avec Jean-René Ruez," *Cultures & Conflicts* 65 (2007), para. 17.

Nations Peace Implementation Force (IFOR) and instead received support from a Norwegian NGO specializing in mine removal to carry out the work.[37]

Analysis of the Bodies

Hiroto Fujiwara, who had worked at the ICTY Prosecutor's Office, conducted detailed research on the ICTY's international criminal investigations. According to him, during the excavation work in Srebrenica, it became clear that one of the forensic officers had falsified data about the burial site, and most of 1997 was spent "proving that all autopsy reports were accurately and properly prepared."[38] The scientific durability of forensic analysis was fundamental to the authority of the ICTY's criminal investigations. Therefore, this was a serious issue.

Once the bodies were excavated, the analysis of physical characteristics was conducted. Forensic anthropologists with specialized knowledge about human bones worked on the analysis of the remains, determining the discovered parts, reconstructing the bodies, and analyzing the physical characteristics indicated by bones and other parts; for example, information such as gender can be obtained from the pelvis, and age from the pubic bone. Then, the cause of death was identified by forensic pathologists with specialized knowledge about the causes of death. Also, to identify the original burial site of the body, land sample surveys were conducted by pollen experts.

In the 1996 autopsy, American forensic pathologist Robert Kirschner played a central role.[39] At this stage, it was verified whether the excavated remains were truly human, when the death occurred, how old the deceased was, what attributes they had (for example, gender, ethnicity, civilian/military), whether the bones showed information related to identification, and how they died.[40] The investigation team collected tissues such as blood and hair on site, as well as potential cloth used for blindfolds and fragments of explosives, and sent these samples to the Netherlands Forensic Institute for analysis. In addition, forensic investigations were conducted using a global network of specialized institutions, such as analyzing the collected shell casings at a research institute in the United States.[41]

Ultimately, after entering the analysis results into the data, the identification was made by comparing it with the physical characteristics and medical information of the missing person during their lifetime. Information about the missing persons, unlike the analysis of the bodies, was obtained through interviews with survivors. The information about the missing persons in Srebrenica was independently collected by the ICRC and PHR, who were searching for the missing persons on site.[42] The

---

37 Stover and Peress, *The Graves*, 147–48.

38 Fujiwara, "International Criminal Investigation by ICTY and Srebrenica," 128.

39 Stover and Peress, *The Graves*, 170; Tom Hundley, "Chicagoan is Tackling Bosnia Forensic Puzzle," *Chicago Tribune*, August 18, 1996.

40 Stover and Peress, *The Graves*, 163.

41 Dean Manning, *Srebrenica Investigation: Summary of Forensic Evidence – Execution Points and Mass Graves*, May 16, 2000.

42 The ICRC conducted an investigation immediately after the massacre, and PHR conducted an independent investigation about a year later. Helge Brunborg, Torkild Hovde Lyngstad, and Henrik

ICRC, as part of its organizational philosophy, does not take on the role of providing evidence in court or as a witness, so activities were carried out for humanitarian purposes, such as collecting and providing information for the remaining families.[43] Nevertheless, the ICRC's list of missing persons, along with PHR's information, became a very important source of information for generating death data.

The Impact of DNA Testing

From 2001 onwards, the forensic investigation was taken over by the International Commission on Missing Persons (ICMP) from the ICTY, and full-scale DNA identification began.[44] The ICMP, as introduced in the previous chapter, is an international organization established under the initiative of US President Clinton at the G7 Summit in 1996, with the aim of investigating the identities of missing persons in the former Yugoslav Wars.[45]

DNA testing, from the late 1980s to the early 1990s, was disputed for its effectiveness in forensic investigations,[46] but by the late 1990s, the controversy had subsided and DNA testing technology rapidly developed, becoming frequently used in crime investigations in developed countries.[47] This DNA testing also played a significant role in the search for missing persons in conflict zones. Why was DNA testing important? For example, in the case of the Srebrenica massacre, as mentioned earlier, many bodies were once buried, then dug up by Serbian military forces and reburied in secondary burial sites, often destroyed and scattered. Therefore, it was extremely difficult to reconstruct a person from the remains. If it is not known whether the scattered remains belong to one person or multiple people, the number of victims is also unknown. However, individual identification of the remains became possible through DNA testing, allowing the discovered parts to be reconstructed.[48] DNA testing also had a significant impact on identity investigations. Before its introduction, identity investigations were conducted through comparisons with personal effects and medical records, but due to lack of data, the work progressed slowly,[49] with DNA

Urdal, "Accounting for Genocide: How Many Were Killed in Srebrenica?" *European Journal of Population* 19, no. 3 (2003): 233–34.

[43] M. Tidball-Binz and U. Hofmeister, "Forensic Archaeology in Humanitarian Contexts; ICRC Action and Recommendations," in *Forensic Archaeology: A Global Perspective*, ed. W. J. Mike Groen, Nicholas Márquez-Grant, and Robert C. Janaway (Chichester, West Sussex: Wiley Blackwell, 2015).

[44] Karadžić Judgment, Trial Chamber, March 24, 2016, para. 5523, 5559.

[45] For ICMP activities, see Ian Hanson, "Forensic Archaeology and the International Commission on Missing Persons: Setting Standards in an Integrated Process," in *Forensic Archaeology: A Global Perspective*, ed. W. J. Mike Groen, Nicholas Márquez-Grant, and Robert C. Janaway (Chichester, West Sussex: Wiley Blackwell, 2015), and ICMP, *Missing Persons*.

[46] Henry Erlich, "In the Beginning: Forensic Applications of DNA Technologies," in *Silent Witness*, ed. Henry Erlich, Eric Stover and Thomas J. White (Oxford: Oxford University Press, 2020), 22.

[47] Samantha Weinberg, *Pointing from the Grave: A True Story of Murder and DNA* (London: Hamish Hamilton, 2003).

[48] Sarah E. Wagner, *To Know Where He Lies: DNA Technology and the Search for Srebrenica's Missing* (Berkeley: University of California Press, 2008), 90.

[49] Ibid., 82.

testing greatly changing this situation. However, to determine identity, DNA data from the relatives of the people on the missing persons list was necessary, requiring the enormous task of requesting this from a large number of people.[50]

The ICMP investigated 1,368 suspected burial sites from 2001 to 2008.[51] As a result of their continuous efforts, by the end of 2014, nearly 7,000 identity investigations related to the Srebrenica massacre had been completed.[52] Thus, scientifically durable data was accumulated, and as it was reported by local media, the theory advocated by Serbian political forces that "the deaths in Srebrenica were the result of infighting within the Bosnian army" was denied.[53]

However, during the investigation, the families of the missing persons could not easily accept the death of their loved ones. For example, in February 1996, hundreds of women who received death certificates of the missing persons from the ICRC stormed the ICRC headquarters, venting their anger at the ICRC's death certificate program and not accepting being unilaterally told of the death without even seeing the body.[54] Also, when the ICMP collected DNA sample data from the remaining families, it was difficult to persuade the families to provide samples, with the provision not compulsory, but voluntary. They could not consider the possibility that their loved ones had died without seeing the body.[55]

Forensic Data as Evidence in Court

Those involved in the Srebrenica massacre could potentially be charged with multiple crimes under international law: first, crimes in violation of the 1949 Geneva Conventions (Article 2 of the ICTY Statute); second, crimes in violation of international humanitarian law and customary law (Article 3 of the same); third, crimes against humanity (Article 5 of the same); and fourth, genocide (Article 4 of the same). The requirements for these crimes to be established are different, but the purpose of this book is not to examine such issues under international law. It is an analysis of the function and role that forensic data played in court.

In relation to forensic data, what is important is how the attributes of the deceased (such as ethnicity and distinction between civilians/combatants) and the cause of death are connected to the above crimes. The first, second, and third crimes question whether the deceased was a civilian, while the fourth crime questions the ethnicity of the deceased. The cause of death is related to all crimes, but what is particularly

---

[50] Ibid., 118.

[51] ICMP, *Missing Persons*, 57–58.

[52] Ibid., 64, 96.

[53] Lara J. Nettelfield and Sarah Wagner, *Srebrenica in the Aftermath of Genocide* (Cambridge: Cambridge University Press, 2014), 261–62.

[54] Stover and Peress, *The Graves*, 196.

[55] ""Relatives will never believe in the death of a loved one if they do not see the body." Kathryne Bomberger, Director of the International Commission on Missing Persons, tells how they will be searched in Ukraine — an interview," Babel, June 14, 2022, https://babel.ua/en/texts/79942-relatives-will-never-believe-in-the-death-of-a-loved-one-if-they-do-not-see-the-body-kathryne-bomberger-director-of-the-international-commission-on-missing-persons-tells-how-they-will-be-searched-in-u.

important is whether the death was a result of combat or whether the person was executed in a defenseless state.

Accordingly, our attention should be directed towards elucidating how the matter of "attributes as civilians" and the cause of death of those implicated in the Srebrenica massacre were substantiated in court through forensic data. For this purpose, we will examine two trial cases that were also covered in Chap. 5. One is the trial of Radislav Krstić, who served as the commander of the Drina Corps, a Serbian military force accused of carrying out the massacre in Srebrenica. The other is the trial of Radovan Karadžić, who was the first president of the Republika Srpska and the supreme commander of the Republika Srpska army.

Krstić Trial

In this trial, in addition to the submission of reports, several experts involved in forensic investigations testified as witnesses. Specifically, these included the chief investigator Jean-René Ruez, investigator Dean Manning from the Australian police, Australian forensic archaeologist Richard Wright, forensic anthropologist William Haglund, Peruvian forensic anthropologist Jose Baraybar, Scottish forensic pathologist John Clark, and Australian forensic pathologist Christopher Lawrence.[56] The experts were first questioned about their degrees, research, specialties, and backgrounds to confirm whether they were qualified as experts, that is, whether they were suitable individuals to represent the knowledge of forensic science. They were then asked to explain their work and investigation data at the ICTY one by one.

In the case of the bodies related to Srebrenica, most of the causes of death were gunshot wounds, but the cords that bound the hands and the blindfolds were discussed as important evidence.[57] These suggested the possibility that the deceased were killed in a defenseless state, indicating that the cause of death was not suicide or combat, but execution.[58] Also, there were hardly any wounds that would have been caused by combat on the bodies, and many were shot from behind, not from the front. These factors further increased the possibility of execution.[59] However, many of the experts refrained from interpreting whether executions had taken place, testifying only about the condition of the remains and artifacts. They also pointed out that scientifically, it was impossible to completely rule out the possibility of death due to combat.[60] They merely presented the bundle of possibilities derived from forensic science.

In this trial, determining whether the deceased were civilians was also a crucial issue, and in many cases, the clues were the deceased's belongings. However, the experts stated that determining whether the deceased were civilians was beyond their authority, and they only testified about the nature of the found artifacts. According

---

[56] ICTY, Prosecutor v. Krstić (Case No. IT–98–33), Transcript (May 26, 2000–May 31, 2000), 3532–4034.

[57] This point has been a topic of discussion many times in the testimony of a series of experts. See Krstić Transcript (May 26, 2000–May 31, 2000), 3532–4034.

[58] For example, Krstić Transcript, May 29, 2000, 3765, 3769.

[59] For example, Krstić Transcript, May 31, 2000, 3940, 3958.

[60] For example, Krstić Transcript, May 30, 2000, 3858–3859.

to their testimonies, hardly any military uniforms were found among the artifacts, and most were clothes that ordinary citizens would wear in their daily lives.[61]

How was the verdict reached? In the first trial, it was determined that the victims primarily died by execution, with data collected and submitted by forensic experts and other specialists being the basis for this. Specifically, blindfolds were found on at least 448 bodies, and 423 cords that appeared to have been used to bind hands and other body parts were discovered. Furthermore, there were no wounds that would likely be caused by combat, and it was determined that the victims had died from gunshot wounds. Also, these forensic data matched the testimonies of the survivors, and it could be interpreted that the Serbian military forces had gone to the trouble of re-burying the bodies from the primary burial sites to secondary ones, seemingly in an attempt to conceal evidence.[62] From these findings, the verdict was guilty of violations of international humanitarian law and wartime customs, crimes against humanity, and genocide.

The Karadzic Trial

In the trial of Karadzic, as in the previous trials including the Krstic trial, a large number of forensic data such as reports and expert testimonies were used. However, in the trial, two points were confirmed regarding the scientific validity of the forensic investigation by the ICTY. The first was the scientific validity of Haglund's forensic investigation. Since his previous forensic investigation in Rwanda had been an issue at the International Criminal Tribunal for Rwanda (ICTR), the ICTY also confirmed whether there were no flaws in his investigation method.[63] The second was that it was problematic that forensic pathologist Kirschner revised the autopsy report without consulting other pathologists and members.[64]

While examining these issues related to scientific validity, the evidence and testimonies presented in the Krstic trial were cited many times in this trial as well. Here, too, the blindfolds and cords that had been used to bind the arms of the bodies became one of the points of contention.[65] The ICTY's forensic experts argued that the interpretation that the cords were blindfolds was the most plausible based on the condition of the cloth and the bodies.[66] The Karadzic side brought in a forensic expert separate from the ICTY's forensic investigation team as a witness and presented a different interpretation of the death data. For example, they argued that the cloth claimed to be a blindfold was merely a part of clothing, or a bandana with religious significance for the soldiers.[67]

---

[61] For example, Krstić Transcript, May 30, 2000, 3818, 3857, 3875.

[62] ICTY, Prosecutor v. Krstić (Case No. IT-98-33), Judgment, Trial Chamber, August 2, 2001, para. 75–78.

[63] ICTY, Prosecutor v. Karadžić (Case IT-95-5/18-T), Transcript, January 30, 2012, 23879.

[64] Karadžić Transcript, January 30, 2012, 23881–23883.

[65] For Haglund's testimony on this point, see Karadžić Transcript (January 30, 2012–January 31, 2012), and for Clark's testimony, see Karadžić Transcript (January 10, 2012-January11, 2012).

[66] Karadžić Transcript, January 31, 2012, 23914–23915, 23947–23948.

[67] Karadžić Transcript, July 23, 2013, 41755.

In the trial's judgment, the condition of such bodies and personal effects was interpreted as evidence of execution. Furthermore, based on the report, it was recognized that many of the deceased were civilians. Thus, Karadzic was found guilty of crimes against international humanitarian law and customary law, crimes against humanity, and genocide.[68] In this way, the activities of the international network of forensic experts had a significant impact on the establishment of the ICTY and the trials at the ICTY. Forensic data was scientifically durable and tended to be recognized as legal evidence.

However, not all people in the former Yugoslavia accepted such trials based on scientific evidence. In particular, it has been pointed out that the Serbian people often took a negative attitude towards the ICTY, resenting being portrayed unilaterally as perpetrators of the conflict.[69] For them, the problem was the indiscriminate attacks by the Bosnian army over several years before the Srebrenica massacre; they could not accept that this was being ignored in the context of the judgment.[70] Such contexts and structures of war differ somewhat from scientific data. Therefore, in the Republika Srpska, one of the regions constituting Bosnia and Herzegovina, and mainly inhabited by Serbian residents, the Srebrenica Historical Project has been carried out to establish and spread a different interpretation of the Srebrenica incident.[71] Thus, scientific data cannot resolve all discrepancies in the collective memory of war.

6.4 Expansion of the International Commission on Missing Persons

From Natural Disasters to the Ukraine War

The ICMP, which was responsible for the forensic investigation of missing persons and bodies in the former Yugoslav Wars, expanded its scope of activities in 2003 to address the issue of missing persons worldwide. This included not only conflicts but also cases of natural disasters. For example, the ICMP addressed the issue of missing persons through forensic investigations in response to the tsunami caused by the earthquake off Sumatra in 2004 and the damage caused by Hurricane Katrina that hit the United States in 2005.[72] Natural disasters, like wars, have resulted in many cases of missing persons.

---

[68] Karadžić Judgment, Trial Chamber (March 24, 2016), para. 5643–5645.

[69] Laurel E. Fletcher and Harvey M. Weinstein, "A World unto Itself? The Application of International Justice in the Former Yugoslavia," in *My Neighbor, My Enemy: Justice and Community in the Aftermath of Mass Atrocity*, ed. Eric Stover and Harvey M. Weinstein (Cambridge: Cambridge University Press, 2004).

[70] Hiroto Fujiwara, "Collective Memory of Srebrenica" [Japanese] in *Srebrenica Genocide: Lessons and Challenges on its 25th Anniversary* (Tokyo: Toshindo, 2020), 58–61.

[71] Nettelfield and Wagner, *Srebrenica in the Aftermath of Genocide*, 279–81.

[72] https://www.icmp.int/bs/press-releases/2005-successful-year-for-icmp/.

By the end of 2014, an agreement regarding the ICMP[73] was concluded in Brussels, and the ICMP officially gained legal status as an international organization searching for missing persons. The first countries to ratify this agreement were the Netherlands, the United Kingdom, Belgium, Luxembourg, and Sweden. Consequently, the ICMP moved its headquarters from Sarajevo to The Hague in the Netherlands.

In recent years, the ICMP has been working on the search for missing persons in the Syrian conflict. According to the Syrian Network for Human Rights, since 2011, about 10,000 people have gone missing.[74] The ICMP has considered enforced disappearances, arbitrary detention, deaths due to torture and mass executions, forced migration, and ongoing conflicts as possible causes of disappearance. Therefore, the ICMP has been working on building a database of missing persons in cooperation with Syrian civil society organizations.

Also, since the Malaysia Airlines plane was shot down in 2014, the ICMP has been dealing with the issue of missing persons in Ukraine. In this 2014 incident, a Malaysia Airlines passenger plane was shot down, killing all 298 people on board. In response to this incident, the Ukrainian government requested the International Criminal Police Organization (Interpol) to investigate the victims' identities, and the ICMP joined Interpol's investigation team and conducted forensic investigations.[75] Furthermore, in 2022, ICMP was conducting forensic investigations in cooperation with the Ukrainian government on the issue of numerous civilian bodies found near Bucha, a suburb of Kyiv.[76] In November of the same year, it revealed that more than 15,000 people have gone missing in the Ukraine War.[77]

*

In wars, a large number of missing persons and bodies occur, and their investigation becomes necessary, with many countries facing this problem since the nineteenth century. In the late 1970s, during Argentina's Dirty War, civilian groups were formed to search for missing persons and, in the process, a network of forensic experts was formed, which later actively worked in the former Yugoslav Wars. The network of forensic experts was a global one, connecting specialist institutions around the

---

[73] The official name of the agreement is the Agreement on the Status and Functions of the International Commission on Missing Persons.

[74] Syrian Network for Human Rights, *The Ninth Annual Report on Enforced Disappearance in Syria on the International Day of the Victims of Enforced Disappearances; There Is No Political Solution without the Disappeared*, August 30, 2020.

[75] INTERPOL, "Interpol Team to Help Identify Victims of Malaysia Airlines Crash," July 18, 2014, https://www.interpol.int/News-and-Events/News/2014/INTERPOL-team-to-help-identify-victims-of-Malaysia-Airlines-crash.

[76] https://www.icmp.int/bs/where-we-work/europe/ukraine/.

[77] https://jp.reuters.com/article/ukraine-crisis-missing-idJPKBN2SE1HI.

world and playing a significant role in the establishment of the ICTY and in its trials. The data they generated was essential in holding those responsible for violations of international law accountable. Furthermore, the ICMP, established during this conflict, became an organization contributing to the issue of missing persons worldwide through forensic investigations, not just in the former Yugoslav Wars. They have been conducting forensic investigations in recent conflicts in Syria and Ukraine as well.

While forensic investigations build solid facts based on scientific durability, we must not forget that the families of the missing and the bereaved cannot easily accept the death of their loved ones, and many Serbs showed a negative attitude towards the ICTY trials. Even if the data underpinning the verdict has scientific durability, if the interpretation of the context and structure of the war presupposed by the verdict is not accepted, the verdict may not gain social credibility. After all, we must always be aware of who and what needs the DAC is designed to meet. Scientific objectivity alone cannot save people and society.

Chapter 7
Chasing Chemical Weapons: War and Chemistry

Contents

In 2012, US President Barack Obama stated that the use of chemical weapons in the conflict was a "red line" for the Assad regime in Syria. The use of chemical weapons is a kind of taboo in today's international society; in fact, the use of chemical weapons is prohibited by several international laws. Nevertheless, unlike nuclear weapons, the line prohibiting the use of chemical weapons has often been crossed. If chemical weapons are used during a war, a global humanitarian network, including the United Nations, begins fact-finding. There have been numerous investigations into the use of chemical weapons by the United Nations and NGOs, and this chapter examines the structure and history of who exactly conducts these investigations and generates war data on chemical weapons.[1] In this book, the term "chemical weapons" refers to substances designed to kill or impair humans or animals using toxic chemicals (and substances in their pre-production stages).

[1] For studies on arms control of chemical weapons, see Michael Crowley, Malcolm Dando, and Lijun Shang, eds., *Preventing Chemical Weapons: Arms Control and Disarmament as the Sciences Converge* (London: The Royal Society of Chemistry, 2018); Nathan E. Busch and Joseph F. Pilat, *The Politics of Weapons Inspections: Assessing WMD Monitoring and Verification Regimes* (Stanford: Stanford University Press, 2017); Alexander Kelle, Kathryn Nixdorff, and Malcolm Dando, *Controlling Biochemical Weapons: Adapting Multilateral Arms Control for the 21st Century* (Basingstoke: Palgrave Macmillan, 2006).

M. Igarashi, *War and Data on Armed Conflicts*, Evidence-Based Approaches to Peace and Conflict Studies 14, https://doi.org/10.1007/978-981-97-6418-1_7

7.1 History of Chemical Weapons Prohibition

In my opinion, the history of international law prohibiting chemical weapons can be traced back to the Strasbourg Agreement of 1675. This agreement, made between France and the Holy Roman Empire, is known for prohibiting the use of poison and poisoned weapons. Furthermore, the use of poison was also prohibited in the Lieber Code, a wartime law drafted by Francis Lieber during the American Civil War (Article 16, Article 70), which was a codification of the wartime customary law in Europe at the time. Therefore, it can be considered that by this point, an international norm had already been established in Europe to avoid the use of poison during wartime. This became even more clear with the Hague Convention of 1899, which was adopted at the first International Peace Conference held in Hague. In its Article 23, the use of poison and poisoned weapons is prohibited.[2]

While the use of poison in wartime was prohibited in this way, the science and technology related to chemical weapons gradually developed. For example, chlorine, which was used as a poison gas weapon in World War I, was discovered at the end of the eighteenth century. In the early nineteenth century, chemical substances such as phosgene and chloropicrin, which were later used as chemical weapons, were discovered in Britain. However, these were not discovered with the intention of creating chemical weapons from the start.

Changes in World War I

The taboo regarding chemical weapons was clearly broken in World War I. The person who triggered this was Fritz Haber, a German chemist. Haber was born in 1868 into a Jewish family in Prussia, with his most famous achievement as a chemist the development of the Haber–Bosch process, which synthesizes ammonia from nitrogen in the air. This was a revolutionary discovery for the production of fertilizers necessary for agriculture, for which Haber received the Nobel Prize in Chemistry.[3]

Haber also left his name in history for his negative achievement of developing chemical weapons for the German army. First, he devised a strategy of filling chlorine into gas cylinders and releasing it on the battlefield. However, not only did he devise this, he also proposed the idea to the German army and brought it to fruition.[4] As is well known, World War I was fought mainly in trenches, and chlorine gas was well suited to the structure of the trenches. Trenches were holes or ditches dug to protect

---

[2] Jonathan B. Tucker, *War of Nerves: Chemical Warfare from World War I to al-Qaeda* (New York: Pantheon Books, 2006), Ch. 1. Also, refer to the historical context as told by the OPCW, https://www.opcw.org/about-us/history.

[3] Thomas Hager, *The Alchemy of Air: A Jewish Genius, a Doomed Tycoon, and the Scientific Discovery That Fed the World but Fueled the Rise of Hitler* (New York: Harmony Books, 2008).

[4] Margit Szöllösi-Janze, "The Scientist as Expert: Fritz Haber and German Chemical Warfare During the First World War and Beyond," in *One Hundred Years of Chemical Warfare: Research, Deployment, Consequences*, ed. Bretislav Friedrich, Dieter Hoffmann, Jürgen Renn, Florian Schmaltz, and Martin Wolf (Cham: Springer Open, 2017).

oneself from enemy shells, and chlorine gas, being heavier than air, filled these holes or ditches on the wind, killing the soldiers.

Furthermore, Haber led an organization to research toxic weapons for the German military, involving many scientists in the war effort. He thus contributed to the practical use of mustard gas,[5] which became one of the most used chemical weapons in war. Mustard gas causes pain in the eyes and throat, difficulty breathing, and vomiting by attacking the mucous membranes of the eyes and respiratory system, while also causing severe inflammation with itching and pain when it comes into contact with the skin, resulting in blisters and ulcers. Despite his significant contributions to the German military, Haber, being of Jewish descent, was forced out of public office when the Nazis took power and was forced to flee to the United Kingdom. He ended his life in despair.

From the Establishment of the Geneva Convention to World War II

Chemical weapons were used in earnest in World War I, but after the war, Western countries began efforts to ban them again. As a result, the Geneva Protocol was established in 1925. The formal name of this protocol is the Protocol for the Prohibition of the Use in War of Asphyxiating, Poisonous or Other Gases, and of Bacteriological Methods of Warfare, which banned the use of chemical weapons in war, along with biological weapons. However, this treaty did not restrict the development, production, or possession of chemical weapons.

Contrary to the progress of international law, several colonial empires paved the way for the practical use of chemical weapons. In the Spanish-Moroccan War (Rif War) that broke out in 1921, the Spanish army used phosgene and chloropicrin as weapons from the beginning of the war. Then, in 1924, they finally dropped mustard gas by air raid. Spain did not ratify the Geneva Protocol until 1929, after the end of this colonial war.[6] Italy also extensively used chemical weapons in its colonial wars. During the reconquest of Libya that began in 1922, Italy dropped phosgene by air raid. Furthermore, in the 1930s, it used poison gas weapons, including mustard gas, in colonial wars in various parts of East Africa, such as Ethiopia.[7] Japan was also known for its active use of poison gas weapons, such as in the Sino-Japanese War, as well as in Taiwan.[8]

In addition to practical use, weapons development also advanced. For example, in Germany, deadly nerve gases were invented one after another. Nerve gas is a general term for chemical weapons that contain organophosphorus compounds and can cause

---

[5] Bretislav Friedrich and Jeremiah James, "From Berlin-Dahlem to the Fronts of World War I: The Role of Fritz Haber and His Kaiser Wilhelm Institute in German Chemical Warfare," in *One Hundred Years of Chemical Warfare: Research, Deployment, Consequences*, ed. Bretislav Friedrich, Dieter Hoffmann, Jürgen Renn, Florian Schmaltz and Martin Wolf (Cham: Springer Open, 2017).

[6] Edward M. Spiers, *Agents of War: A History of Chemical and Biological Weapons (Revised and Expanded 2nd Edition)* (London: Reaktion Books Ltd, 2021), 73–74.

[7] Ibid., 75.

[8] See Seiya Matsuno, *Chemical Weapons of the Japanese Army* (Tokyo: Gaifūsha, 2005) [Japanese]; and Yoshiaki Yoshimi, *Chemical Warfare and the Japanese Army* (Tokyo: Iwanami Shoten, 2004) [Japanese].

death in a short time by absorbing only a small amount through the skin or mucous membranes. In 1936, Gerhard Schrader accidentally developed the nerve gas, Tabun (whose name comes from the word "taboo"), with powerful lethal capabilities while trying to develop an insecticide to increase agricultural production. Furthermore, in 1938, he completed the nerve gas Sarin. The German army, in response to these inventions, prepared to mass-produce these chemical weapons and deploy them in actual combat. All that was left was to get permission to use them, but for some reason, Hitler never decided to use them on the battlefield. However, Nazi Germany used a cyanide-based insecticide named Zyklon B to commit mass murder of Jews.[9]

Afterwards, the know-how of chemical weapons spread from Germany to the rest of the world. At the end of World War II, with the collapse of Nazi Germany, the victorious nations collected information on chemical weapons from German officials and began developing nerve gases such as Tabun. With the start of the Cold War, they mass-produced these German-derived chemical weapons in preparation for a new war. In addition, in Britain, VX gas was developed as a new nerve gas,[10] with a supposedly relatively recent example of the use of VX gas seen with the assassination of Kim Jong-nam, the half-brother of North Korea's supreme leader Kim Jong-un. The methods of producing these nerve gases spread to countries in Asia and Africa during the Cold War.

7.2 Fact-Finding by Humanitarian Networks

Yemen Civil War

In the 1960s, a civil war broke out in Yemen, during which chemical weapons were used (see Chap. 4). In 1962, Egypt militarily intervened in this civil war and executed a strategy of dropping chemical weapons from bombers as part of its counter-guerrilla operations. Initially, they used tear gas, but eventually they used phosgene and mustard gas. Prior to this war, under the leadership of President Nasser, Egypt had planned the development of chemical weapons, had related personnel receive technical training in the Soviet Union, and hired West German scientists and technicians who had worked on development in Nazi Germany, accumulating chemical weapons capabilities.[11]

Saudi Arabia also intervened in this civil war, conflicting with Egypt. In July 1963, considering the use of chemical weapons as intolerable, Saudi Arabia accused Egypt of using chemical weapons in Yemen and filed a complaint with UN Secretary-General U Thant. The ICRC also conducted its own investigation and formally protested against Egypt's use of chemical weapons. However, U Thant, while encouraging the establishment of the United Nations Yemen Observation Mission

---

9 Tucker, War of Nerves, Ch. 3.

10 Ibid., Ch. 5–9.

11 Ibid., Ch. 10.

(UNYOM), avoided a direct response to the chemical weapons issue. Ultimately, the UN did not conduct a fact-finding mission on chemical weapons, but in 1969, U Thant submitted a report titled "Chemical and Bacteriological (Biological) Weapons and the Effects of Their Possible Use," urging the consideration of rules to prohibit chemical weapons.[12]

Fact-Finding in the Iran-Iraq War

The humanitarian network centered on the United Nations conducted a full-scale investigation into the wartime use of chemical weapons during the Iran-Iraq War, which took place from 1980 to 1988. In this war, the use of chemical weapons became a major issue, and fact-finding by experts was conducted several times under the leadership of the UN Secretary-General. At that time, tensions between the United States and the Soviet Union were escalating due to the onset of the new Cold War, and the United Nations worked to generate war data on chemical weapons.

One of the underlying causes of the Iran-Iraq War was the Islamic Revolution in Iran in 1979. From the mid-1970s, resentment against the king spread in Iran. When the Islamic leader Khomeini, who was in exile in Paris, began to lead the anti-government movement, the movement progressed towards the overthrow of the monarchy. In 1979, the king fled abroad and Khomeini returned home, finally establishing the Islamic Republic. In Iraq, there was a fear that Iran's ideology and policies might have a negative impact on domestic politics,[13] and from this point on, relations between Iran and Iraq rapidly deteriorated. In addition to these ideological issues, there were also territorial disputes between the two countries. In September 1980, Iraq under the Saddam Hussein regime invaded Iran, and a full-scale armed conflict began. The UN Security Council immediately issued a resolution calling for a ceasefire, but it had little effect and the conflict continued to worsen.

In this war, chemical weapons were primarily used by Iraq. Initially, Iran was pushed back by Iraq's offensive, but later rebounded, resulting in a complete stalemate. In the summer of 1983, after losing part of its Kurdish autonomous region due to Iran's offensive, Iraq used chemical weapons such as mustard gas, which it had been preparing beforehand, against Iranian forces,[14] and continued to use chemical weapons frequently thereafter. As mentioned earlier, the use of chemical weapons was prohibited by the Geneva Protocol of 1925, and Iraq's actions were in violation of it.

In November 1983, Iran appealed to UN Secretary-General Javier Pérez de Cuéllar to address the issue of Iraq's use of chemical weapons and to conduct a fact-finding mission by experts. De Cuéllar, originally a Peruvian diplomat, had just taken office as Secretary-General in 1982. Although de Cuéllar was proactive in fact-finding, there had been no precedent for the UN conducting fact-finding on the wartime

---

[12] United Nations, *Chemical and Bacteriological (Biological) Weapons and the Effects of Their Possible Use* (New York: United Nations, 1969).

[13] Bryan R. Gibson, *Covert Relationship: American Foreign Policy, Intelligence, and the Iran-Iraq War, 1980–1988* (Santa Barbara: Praeger Publisher, 2010), 24–35.

[14] Ibid., 105–106.

use of chemical weapons, and the Security Council did not respond to de Cuéllar's request to embark on the fact-finding mission.[15] Also, at this time, the fact that the United States was in a diplomatic confrontation with Iran over the bombing of the US embassy in Lebanon and was approaching Iraq diplomatically hindered the issue from becoming a point of contention.[16]

Dispatch of Four Experts

In February 1984, when Iraq began to use chemical weapons on a large scale, Western media also began to cover the issue. As a result, even the United States, which sided with Iraq, had no choice but to issue a statement condemning Iraq's use of chemical weapons.[17] The following month, Secretary-General de Cuéllar, on his own initiative, dispatched a team of four medical and military experts to Iran[18] from Sweden, Spain, Australia, and Switzerland, respectively.[19] The purpose of the investigation was to clarify whether chemical weapons were used in Iran and, if used, what type of weapons were used. They also planned to investigate in Iraq, but were denied by the Iraqi government.

The methods of investigating chemical weapons include: (1) interviews with related parties, (2) environmental sample surveys at suspected sites of chemical weapon use, (3) physical investigations into the transportation methods of toxic substances such as missiles, and (4) medical investigations of affected patients or corpses (for example, in addition to symptom analysis, blood and urine analysis). When all these data are gathered, it becomes clear what kind of chemical substances were transported by what means, when, and what kind of damage they caused to whom. The United Nations investigation team in 1984 implemented these investigation methods in Iran.

Needless to say, it was difficult to conduct all these investigations with only four experts. For example, even for a single sample survey, it was necessary to analyze chemical substances at research institutions but, at that time, there was no such facility at the United Nations. In this investigation, the collected substances were thus sent to the Swedish National Defense Research Institute (now the Swedish Defense Research Agency) and the Swiss AC Research Institute for analysis.[20] Even in fact-finding on chemical weapons, a global network of specialized institutions is essential.

On March 21, 1984, the expert team submitted the results of interviews, sample collection surveys, and clinical examinations of victims in Iran to the UN Secretary-General as a fact-finding report. The report concluded that chemical weapons such as

---

[15] Ibid., 108.

[16] Ibid., 94.

[17] Ibid., 127.

[18] For the movements within the United Nations leading up to the start of the investigation, see Joost R. Hiltermann, *A Poisonous Affair: America, Iraq, and the Gassing of Halabja* (Cambridge: Cambridge University Press, 2007), 58–59.

[19] S/16433, March 26, 1984, para. 5.

[20] Ibid., Appendix II–VI.

mustard gas and tabun had been used through aerial bombing in the investigation area in Iran. However, whether the Iraqi army was the user was outside the scope of the investigation and was not mentioned.[21] Generally speaking, in the issue of wartime use of chemical weapons, the identification of the user and legal responsibility are the most political issues, so they are often not dealt with in fact-finding.

Iran tried to make the use of chemical weapons an issue at the UN Commission on Human Rights (CHR) as well. The UN did not have an organization that constantly monitored international humanitarian law, and the CHR was effectively taking on that function. However, this attempt was thwarted by the United States, which supported Iraq.[22] In the Security Council, the United Kingdom and the Netherlands moved to issue a resolution condemning Iraq's use of chemical weapons, leading to a Security Council Presidential statement on March 30. However, even in this Security Council Presidential statement, Iraq was not named, and it only condemned the use of chemical weapons.[23]

Large-Scale Usage by Iraq

In February 1986, when the al-Faw Peninsula, which was Iraqi territory, was occupied by an Iranian offensive, Iraq responded by using chemical weapons on a large scale. In response to this, Secretary-General de Cuellar dispatched the same team of four experts for a second investigation. On March 7, a report was submitted to the Secretary-General and, for the first time, the use of chemical weapons by the Iraqi army was publicly acknowledged, which was based on new evidence, such as testimonies from captured Iraqi soldiers.[24] The Iraqi government claimed that the Iranian army had used chemical weapons, as Iraqi soldiers were also victims, but this was not accepted.[25] In response to this, the Iraqi army was specifically condemned in the Security Council Presidential statement on March 21,[26] which led to Iraq in turn responding by strongly objecting, claiming that the UN's stance was too unbalanced.[27]

In April 1987, the Iraqi army used chemical weapons on a large scale against Iran and Kurdish settlements within Iraq, which continued until a ceasefire in 1988. In response to the Kurdish forces attacking on the side of Iran during the Iran-Iraq War, Iraq attacked the Kurds with chemical weapons, intentionally targeting not only the military but also civilians. In response, Secretary-General de Cuellar dispatched a team of four experts again. In their investigation, in addition to Iran, local investigations could be conducted in Iraq. The report pointed out the use of chemical weapons against Iranian civilians,[28] but the damage to the Kurds within

[21] Ibid., Annex, para. 35.

[22] Hiltermann, *A Poisonous Affair*, 52.

[23] S/16454, March 30, 1984.

[24] S/17911, March 12, 1986, Annex, para. 56.

[25] Hiltermann, *A Poisonous Affair*, 72.

[26] S/17932, March 21, 1986.

[27] S/17934, March 23, 1986.

[28] S/18852, May 8, 1987, Annex, para. 64.

Iraq was considered outside the scope of the Geneva Conventions because it was a domestic issue, and was not included in the report.[29] The United States, while condemning Iraq, also claimed that Iran was using chemical weapons.[30]

Afterwards, due to opposition from Iraq and Turkey, the United Nations was unable to conduct a fact-finding investigation into the harm done to the Kurds in northern Iraq. Therefore, the NGO Physicians for Human Rights (PHR) investigated, dispatching three doctors to Turkey in October 1988, where they conducted interviews and medical examinations, as well as video recording, at refugee camps regarding chemical weapon attacks. As a result of the investigation, it was concluded that on August 25, 1988, Iraqi aircraft attacked Kurdish villages in northern Iraq with bombs filled with poison gas.[31]

Institutional Development of the Investigation

As a result of these series of events, the United Nations institutionalized the Secretary-General's authority to investigate chemical weapons issues. In November 1987, Resolution 42/37C was adopted at the UN General Assembly, and in August 1988, Resolution 620 was adopted at the Security Council. These resolutions allowed the Secretary-General to conduct fact-finding investigations at his own discretion when he received reports indicating the possible use of chemical weapons. A quarter of a century later, investigations into the use of chemical weapons in the Syrian conflict would be conducted based on these systems.

The United States, having allowed Iraq's use of chemical weapons in the Iran-Iraq War, suffered the consequences in the Gulf War. In August 1990, when Iraq began invading and occupying Kuwait, the UN Security Council issued a resolution for Iraq's withdrawal, but Iraq did not comply. Therefore, in January 1991, a multinational force led by the United States began attacking Iraq based on the Security Council resolution. At this time, the United States feared that Iraq would counter with chemical weapons and was forced to take measures against it. Although the Iraqi military did not end up using chemical weapons, it became clear that the issue of chemical weapons was not limited to conflicts between developing countries.[32] In May 1991, the United Nations established the United Nations Special Commission (UNSCOM) to monitor and promote Iraq's disarmament.

Multilateral negotiations for a treaty prohibiting the development, production, storage, and use of chemical weapons also intensified in response to the Iran-Iraq War and the Gulf War. Although the negotiations had already begun in the 1980s at the UN Disarmament Commission, it was after these two wars that major powers, including the United States, finally became serious about the issue. In November 1992, the Convention on the Prohibition of the Development, Production, Stockpiling and Use of Chemical Weapons and on their Destruction (the Chemical Weapons Convention) was adopted at the UN General Assembly and came into effect five years later. Along

[29] Hiltermann, *A Poisonous Affair*, 98.

[30] Gibson, *Covert Relationship*, 212.

[31] Physicians for Human Rights, *Winds of Death: Iraq's Use of Poison Gas* (February 1989).

[32] Tucker, *War of Nerves*, Ch. 15.

with this, the Organisation for the Prohibition of Chemical Weapons (OPCW) was established, which would primarily handle the subsequent investigation of chemical weapons issues.

7.3 Confusion Surrounding Data on Armed Conflicts

Controversy Over the Investigation of Chemical Weapons

A humanitarian network was established to conduct investigations on chemical weapons. However, no matter how scientifically durable the data provided by the humanitarian network is, data on chemical weapons, especially data on their use, is highly political and therefore often sparks major controversies. Various data on the use of chemical weapons were mixed and flying around, causing confusion during the Syrian conflict that occurred in 2011.

In March 2011, peaceful protests against the Assad regime broke out in major cities of Syria, with security forces killing dozens of citizens in an attempt to suppress the spread of the movement. The protest movement expanded further, eventually leading to armed clashes between the regime and the opposition. As the conflict intensified, damage believed to be caused by chemical weapons occurred in various places. This, coupled with the potential for US military intervention, led to the world being swayed by data on the use of chemical weapons. In the Syrian conflict, investigations into the use of chemical weapons were conducted many times, but here we will focus on the analysis of cases where controversy arose over the methods of investigation and data on the use of chemical weapons.

The Start of Chemical Weapons Investigation

The Syrian government had been developing chemical weapons since the 1980s. According to an analysis by US intelligence agencies in 1991, Syria probably had bombs filled with the nerve gas sarin at this point.[33] Therefore, it was not surprising that in July 2012, the Syrian government admitted to possessing chemical weapons in a press conference and suggested the possibility of using them against foreign military intervention.[34] The use of chemical weapons became a significant issue when it was linked to US military intervention; about a month after the Syrian government's press conference, US President Obama stated that the use of chemical weapons by the Assad regime would be "crossing a red line." However, this statement had no deterrent effect.

The Independent International Commission of Inquiry established by the Human Rights Council released its investigation report in February 2013. The report stated that the use of chemical weapons in Syria had not been confirmed,[35] but just a month

[33] Spiers, *Agents of War*, 153–55.

[34] Neil MacFarquhar and Eric Schmitt, "Syria Threatens Chemical Attack on Foreign Force," *New York Times*, July 23, 2012.

[35] A/HRC/22/59, February 5, 2013, para. 21.

later, the use of chemical weapons was reported in the city of Khan al-Assal, near Aleppo.[36] According to a later report by the United Nations, twenty-five people died and one hundred and ten were injured in this incident.[37] Furthermore, there were reports of chemical weapons being used in the Saraqib region of Idlib province at the end of April.[38] In mid-June, the Obama administration expressed the view that these incidents crossed the red line, but the possibility of military intervention was unclear.[39]

The investigation by the United Nations began in response to the incident in Khan al-Assal in March. That same month, UN Secretary-General Ban Ki-moon also decided to establish an independent investigation team on the issue of chemical weapons in Syria. As mentioned in the previous section, as a result of the Iran-Iraq War in the 1980s, the Secretary-General had his own investigative authority. Furthermore, from the mid-2000s, the Secretary-General's ability to investigate chemical weapons issues was further strengthened by building a global network of research institutions.[40] In that sense, the investigation in Syria can be seen to have been undertaken with full readiness.

Angela Kane, the UN High Representative for Disarmament Affairs, was appointed as the head of the investigation, and a team of chemical weapons experts from around the world was assembled. The team leader was Åke Sellström, a Swedish chemical weapons expert who served as the head of the inspection team of the United Nations Special Commission on Disarmament (UNSCOM) from 1994 to 2000.[41] However, the investigation did not go as planned; for some time after the start of the activities, the cooperation of the Syrian government could not be obtained, and time passed without being able to conduct an investigation on the ground. It was only in June of 2013 that the team had the opportunity to autopsy the body of a woman who died in the attack on the Saraqib region in Turkey and were able to collect the first data on the deceased. As a result of the analysis, the investigation team concluded that her death was due to the chemical weapon sarin.[42]

---

[36] Martin Chulov, "Syria Attacks Involved Chemical Weapons, Rebels and Regime Claim," *The Guardian*, March 19, 2013.

[37] A/68/663–S/2013/735, December 13, 2013, para. 5.

[38] Ian Pannell, "Syria Crisis: "Strong Evidence" of Chemical Attacks, in Saraqeb," *BBC News*, May 16, 2013, https://www.bbc.com/news/world-middle-east-22551892.

[39] Ian Black, "Syria: What Is on The Other Side of Barack Obama's Red Line?" *The Guardian*, June 14, 2013.

[40] Michael Crowley, "United Nations Mechanisms to Combat the Development, Acquisition and Use of Chemical Weapons," in *Preventing Chemical Weapons: Arms Control and Disarmament as the Sciences Converge*, ed. Michael Crowley, Malcolm Dando, and Lijun Shang (London: The Royal Society of Chemistry, 2018).

[41] Åke Sellström, "Lessons from Weapons Inspections in Iraq and Syria," *AJIL Unbound* 115 (2021): 95.

[42] A/68/663–S/2013/735, December 13, 2013, para. 27–32; Joby Warrick, *Red Line: The Unravelling of Syria and the Race to Destroy the Most Dangerous Arsenal in the World* (London: Transworld Publishers, 2020), 30–32.

The Incident in Ghouta

Shortly after concrete evidence was raised, the Syrian government announced its acceptance of an investigation team. A total of twenty staff members, composed of officials including WHO, OPCW, and security experts, made their way into Damascus by land from Lebanon on August 18. However, for a while after that, the investigation team was again held back by the Syrian government. But in the early hours of August 21, despite the presence of the investigation team, a large-scale chemical weapons attack occurred in the town of Ghouta near Damascus, and the situation changed dramatically. Once a temporary ceasefire was agreed upon, an on-site investigation was finally realized.[43]

In response to the incident in Ghouta, the US government finally began preparations for an attack on Syria. However, since the implementation of the attack required the departure of the UN investigation team, the US government asked the UN to leave. However, Secretary-General Ban insisted on the need for the continuation and completion of the investigation and defended the activities of the investigation team. Although the US government put pressure on the UN, it eventually conceded, and the investigation continued.[44]

The investigation team, dodging threats and pressure from both the government and anti-government sides, conducted interviews with survivors and witnesses in multiple cities, collected environmental samples, and conducted clinical examinations of survivors.[45] Taking the analysis of these environmental samples as an example, it can be seen that the OPCW's scientific analysis process was conducted under very strict procedures. The samples collected by the investigation team were sent to the OPCW laboratory in Rijswijk, the Netherlands, under UN supervision. There, the samples were classified and organized, sent to multiple OPCW-designated research facilities, and analyzed according to various regulations.[46]

The first report thus produced was released on September 16, 2013, which concluded that the chemical weapon sarin was used in the incident in Ghouta on August 21. However, it did not specify the user or the location of legal responsibility, as these were outside its jurisdiction,[47] but a careful reading of the supplementary materials to the report suggested to those with expert knowledge that it could be interpreted as implying the responsibility of the Syrian government. For example, in the analysis of the rockets that carried the chemical weapons, the direction from which they were presumed to have been launched was determined, and on the map, in that direction, there was a military base of the Syrian government.[48] However, this report did not include any maps, and it was only by comparing it with maps in recently published reports, such as those by Human Rights Watch, that its meaning

---

43 A/68/663–S/2013/735, December 13, 2013, para. 33–36; Warrick, *Red Line*, 59–71.

44 Warrick, *Red Line*, 72–83.

45 A/67/997–S/2013/553, September 16, 2013.

46 A/68/663–S/2013/735, December 13, 2013, para. 40.

47 A/67/997–S/2013/553, September 16, 2013, para. 27–28.

48 Ibid., Appendix 5; Warrick, *Red Line*, 128.

could finally be understood. Furthermore, the analysis of the chemical weapons used revealed the detection of hexamethylenetetramine, which is used in Syria's unique method of producing sarin.[49] This would be understandable to those with some knowledge of sarin production methods, but for others, it would be just another analysis result.

Condemnation of Syria and Russia's Mediation

There was criticism of the Syrian government from various quarters regarding this Ghouta incident. Just before the OPCW report was released, Human Rights Watch published a report on Ghouta, stating that the Syrian government had used chemical weapons and that the possibility of them being used by anti-government forces was minimal.[50] The basis for this was that the weapons used were of a type only used by the Syrian government, the locations targeted were areas controlled by anti-government forces, the areas from which the weapons were presumed to have been launched were controlled by the government, and the pattern of attack matched that of the government's previous actions. The United States also pursued the responsibility of the Syrian government based on independently collected information.[51] In response to these condemnations, President Assad completely denied responsibility for the use of chemical weapons in the Ghouta incident in an interview with an American television station.[52]

Even if the Syrian government used chemical weapons, what legal responsibility can be said to exist? At this point, Syria was not yet a signatory to the Chemical Weapons Convention, but it was a signatory to the Geneva Protocol. The problem is that the Syrian conflict is a civil war, and the Geneva Protocol does not cover the use of chemical weapons in civil wars.[53] However, in September 2013, the UN Security Council adopted Resolution 2118, which considered the use of chemical weapons a violation of international law, which is interpreted as a judgment based on customary law.[54]

However, the situation converged in an unexpected direction. Russia proposed to the United States a plan to dispose of Syria's chemical weapons, which the United States accepted. As a result, the Syrian government agreed to dispose of its chemical weapons[55] and, subsequently, ratified the Chemical Weapons Convention, beginning the work of disposing the chemical weapons. As a result, the possibility of military

---

[49] A/67/997–S/2013/553, September 16, 2013, Appendix 7; Warrick, *Red Line*, 128.

[50] Human Rights Watch, *Attacks on Goutta: Analysis of Alleged Use of Chemical Weapons in Syria*, September 10, 2013.

[51] David Jolly, Scott Sayare, and Rick Gladstone, "U.S. Releases Detailed Intelligence on Syrian Chemical Attack," *The New York Times*, August 30, 2013.

[52] Domic Rushe, "Assad Tells Charlie Rose No Evidence He Is Responsible for Syria Chemical Attack," *The Guardian*, September 8, 2013.

[53] Masahiko Asada, *The Use of Chemical Weapons and International Law: The Case of Syria* (Tokyo: Tohshindo, 2022) [Japanese], 11.

[54] Ibid., 34–35.

[55] Michael R. Gordon, "U.S. and Russia Reach Deal to Destroy Syria's Chemical Arms," *The New York Times*, September 14, 2013.

intervention by the United States also disappeared. The OPCW investigation team conducted additional investigations and in December 2013, released their final report on the use of chemical weapons in various regions, including Ghouta. However, the report did not hold the Syrian government responsible.[56]

Criticism and Rebuttal to the Report

However, the controversy surrounding this incident continues. Seymour Hersh, a world-renowned American journalist, claimed that the Syrian government did not use chemical weapons, and the real culprits were the anti-government forces supported by Turkey. Hersh is known for exposing the My Lai Massacre during the Vietnam War, for which he won the Pulitzer Prize, and his article, therefore, attracted a lot of attention. According to Hersh, the British intelligence agency obtained and analyzed a sample of sarin used in Syria, which did not match that of the Syrian army. Furthermore, he claimed that the al-Nusra Front, a representative anti-government force, had the ability to produce sarin, and the incident in Ghouta was either caused by the al-Nusra Front or by Turkey to make it appear as if the Syrian government was responsible.[57] These claims were based on testimonies Hersh obtained from related parties.

Furthermore, in support of Hersh's claims, two experts, Richard Lloyd and Theodore A. Postol, disputed the analysis results of organizations such as Human Rights Watch. Lloyd served as an inspector for the United Nations Monitoring, Verification and Inspection Commission (UNMOVIC), established in 1999 to monitor the disposal of Iraq's weapons of mass destruction, and Postol was a researcher at the Massachusetts Institute of Technology. According to them, the range of the missile believed to have carried the sarin could be calculated to be shorter than the data pointed out by Human Rights Watch and others, suggesting that it may not have been launched from areas controlled by the Syrian government.[58]

The organization that launched a counter-argument against this was not Human Rights Watch or OPCW, but a non-governmental organization called Bellingcat. The founder of Bellingcat is a British man named Eliot Higgins, who was originally just an ordinary citizen engrossed in online gaming. However, he became fascinated when he started researching the Libyan conflict on the internet, and now is a world-renowned figure as a representative of a non-governmental organization that determines various facts related to armed conflicts from open sources published on the internet.

Bellingcat is an information organization in which volunteers from the general public participate. It is not supported by any specific group, and Higgins himself introduces Bellingcat as "an intelligence agency for the people."[59] Although it tends to

[56] A/68/663–S/2013/735, December 13, 2013, para. 108–122.

[57] Seymour Hersh, "The Red Line and the Rat Line," *London Review of Books* 36, no. 8 (April 11, 2014).

[58] Richard Lloyd and Theodore A. Postol, "Possible Implications of Faulty US Technical Intelligence in the Damascus Nerve Agent Attack of August 21, 2013," January 14, 2014, https://www.documentcloud.org/documents/1006045-possible-implications-of-bad-intelligence.

[59] Eliot Higgins, *We Are Bellingcat: An Intelligence Agency for the People* (London: Bloomsbury, 2021), 8.

defend (political) liberalism and democracy, it does not subscribe to the extreme openness of organizations like WikiLeaks, which believe that all information should be made public. Bellingcat's most well-known achievement is its activity related to the Malaysia Airlines plane shooting incident that occurred in July 2014 where, through a thorough analysis of open sources, it identified and proved that the Russian military was the perpetrator of this shooting (as a result, they became a target of Russia). However, the investigation into the Syrian conflict was what brought Bellingcat into the spotlight. Using countless pieces of information on the internet such as video sites, SNS, maps, etc., they confirmed one after another the facts about the conflict that were not reported, such as the history of the weapons used by the anti-government forces.[60]

Higgins and others pointed out in *The Guardian* that Hersh's argument was full of holes. Regarding the range of the missile in question, an analysis of the report by ANNA News, a pro-Russian media, revealed that the Syrian government forces had recaptured a two-kilometer range area from the anti-government forces by the day the chemical weapons were launched. Therefore, even if this range is correct, the possibility of the Syrian government forces being responsible cannot be denied. Furthermore, in response to Hersh's claim that the al-Nusra Front produced sarin in Aleppo with Turkey's support, they countered that sarin is not something that can be easily produced and requires large facilities and logistics, which Hersh did not discuss.[61]

What is Certain, What is Uncertain

Which claim is correct? Did the Syrian government forces launch sarin with missiles, or did the anti-government forces carry out a false flag operation to make it look like the work of the Syrian government forces? The experts' discussions became very technical, making it difficult to make a quick judgment. As one commentator pointed out, major Western media actively adopted the narrative that the Syrian government was the perpetrator of the Ghouta incident.[62]

If we organize the (English-speaking) controversy so far, what is certain at least is that the nerve gas sarin was used in Syria, with no durable scientific rebuttal to this. The OPCW's analysis procedure is strict, making it difficult to undermine. What about the perpetrator? The OPCW does not have the authority to identify the perpetrator, so it says almost nothing. In the controversy introduced earlier, the evidence presented by Human Rights Watch and Bellingcat has not been completely refuted; in that sense, it can be judged that the Syrian government is likely to be the perpetrator of the Ghouta incident. However, it cannot be said that the false flag operation theory is completely impossible.

---

[60] David Patrikarakos, *War in 140 Characters: How Social Media Is Reshaping Conflict in the Twenty-First Century* (New York: Basic Books, 2017), Ch. 8.

[61] Eliot Higgins and Dan Kaszeta, "It's Clear That Turkey Was Not Involved in The Chemical Attack on Syria," *The Guardian*, April 22, 2014.

[62] Ben Cole, *The Syrian Information and Propaganda War* (Cham: Palgrave Macmillan Cham, 2022), 196.

The Incident in Douma in 2018

In 2014, when the use of chemical weapons in the Syrian conflict was reported again, a joint investigation mechanism of the UN and OPCW was established in 2015, which later reported the use of chemical weapons by the Syrian government and the Islamic State (ISIL) from 2014 to 2016.[63] However, the possibility of US intervention was almost gone, and the issue of chemical weapons was no longer a major issue in the international community. As interest in Syria waned, the chemical weapons incident in Douma in 2018 suddenly drew attention to the structure of war data generation.

On the afternoon of April 7, 2018, numerous reports of the use of chemical weapons in Douma were circulated on SNS and other platforms. That night, attacks were carried out by the Syrian government forces and others, resulting in the deaths of about 40–70 people. While the anti-government forces condemned the use of chemical weapons by the Syrian government forces, the Syrian government denied the use. Subsequently, with the agreement of the Syrian government, it was decided to dispatch the OPCW's fact-finding team.[64] The United States, the United Kingdom, and France believed that the Syrian government was the perpetrator of this incident, and on April 13, they carried out a large-scale air raid on the Syrian government's chemical weapons-related facilities.

Amid concerns about the worsening situation in Syria, the OPCW pre-examined the credibility of information on the internet, and based on information deemed reliable, dispatched a team of nine inspectors and two interpreters to the site to investigate.[65] As in previous cases, the OPCW conducted sample surveys and other procedures and, after a series of investigations, issued an interim report in July 2018 and a final report in March of the following year. In its final report, the OPCW pointed out that no traces of organophosphorus nerve gas were found in the field investigation, and what was found was a substance related to chlorine gas. However, the report, combined with the results of medical investigations, did not state that there was definitive evidence from the sample survey that chlorine gas was used, and only concluded that there was a high possibility of this.[66] The physical evidence was cylinders found at two sites, which were speculated to have released chlorine gas after falling from a high place, with the release of chlorine gas by cylinders a classic method reminiscent of German attacks in World War I. The fact-finding team, using computer modeling, calculated how the cylinders fell, at what speed, and what trajectory.[67] However, the OPCW's conclusion is only about what happened, not who the perpetrator is.

---

[63] Asada, *The Use of Chemical Weapons and International Law*, 54–56.

[64] S/1645/2018, July 6, 2018, para. 3.1–3.4.

[65] Ibid., para. 5.1–5.2.

[66] S/1731/2019, March 1, 2019.

[67] Ibid.

Internal Whistleblowing and Rebuttal

This report suddenly attracted attention, with the trigger the appearance of an internal whistleblower from the OPCW. In May 2019, the Working Group on Syria, Propaganda, and Media, composed of British and American researchers and journalists, published a report by an OPCW technical staff (later identified as Ian Henderson) dated February 2019.[68] This report pointed out that the analysis results of the local investigation did not confirm the fact that the two cylinders were dropped from an aircraft to each place but, rather, they might have been intentionally placed there by someone, in other words, it might have been a false flag operation.[69]

In addition to Henderson, another technical staff member (later identified as Brendan Wheelan) moved to blow the whistle. Between November and December 2019, WikiLeaks released four pieces of confidential information from the OPCW, including internal emails. These emails were sent by Wheelan to senior OPCW officials in June 2018, protesting that the results of the scientific and technical analysis on the ground were not reflected in the interim report; according to his claim, substances related to chlorine gas were not found at high levels in environmental samples, and the symptoms of the alleged victims did not match.[70] At the end of November, Wheelan was invited to testify at a public hearing held in Brussels, which was attended by renowned experts in international law and arms control, including Richard Falk. There, Wheelan testified that there was not enough evidence of chlorine gas, and claimed that during the creation of the report, the investigation team was under political pressure from the United Kingdom and Turkey, among others, through senior OPCW officials.[71]

In response to these internal whistleblowing actions, the OPCW hardly made any scientific counterarguments. Instead, they claimed that these two individuals were not core members of the OPCW investigation team and that their actions violated the rules of confidential information management. On behalf of the OPCW, it was Bellingcat who scientifically verified and refuted the claims of the two whistleblowers, announcing the detailed results of their review on their own site. First, Bellingcat reiterated that chlorine gas was used at the scene. In the Syrian conflict, chlorine gas has been used many times, and various NGO investigations have acknowledged that it was done by the Syrian government, with the only other use acknowledged by the Islamic State. Wheelan argues that because chlorine is used in everyday life it does not constitute evidence, even though traces of it were found at low levels in the room where the cylinder was found. However, according to the

---

[68] OPCW, "Director-General's Statement on the Report of the Investigation into Possible Breaches of Confidentiality," February 6, 2020, 5.

[69] https://wikileaks.org/opcw-douma/document/20190227-Engineering-assessment-of-two-cylinders-observed-at-the-Douma-incident/20190227-Engineering-assessment-of-two-cylinders-observed-at-the-Douma-incident.pdf.

[70] https://wikileaks.org/opcw-douma/releases/#Internal%20OPCW%20E-Mail.

[71] Jonathan Steele, "The OPCW and Douma: Chemical Weapons Watchdog Accused of Evidence-Tampering by Its Own Inspectors," CounterPunch.org, November 15, 2019; Jefferson Morley, "Why Douma Attack Wasn't A "Managed Massacre,"" *Asia Times*, December 8, 2019.

OPCW investigation, traces of chlorine gas at levels expected when used as a weapon have been found. Moreover, since it was found from all walls and rubble, this does not fall into the category everyday use. The fact that a high concentration of chlorine was found under the cylinder and that the nearby metal had chemically reacted with chlorine after the incident were also considered important evidence,[72] while there were also issues with Henderson's comments about the cylinder, such as calculations of the drop height and the shape of the damaged part of the building. Furthermore, it was argued that there was no basis for the claim that someone deliberately installed the cylinder.[73]

Was the Perpetrator the Syrian Government Forces or the Anti-Government Forces?

Did the Syrian government forces really drop cylinders filled with chlorine gas? Or was it done by the anti-government forces as part of a false flag operation? The claim of a false flag operation essentially suggested that the anti-government forces fabricated the Syrian government's gas attack, thereby provoking airstrikes by the United Kingdom and the United States. The OPCW's argument was merely speculating about what happened, not discussing who the perpetrator was.

Ultimately, from the series of discussions, there is almost no evidence found for a false flag operation. Also, the fact that some kind of poison gas was used and victims were produced has not been fundamentally overturned. In that respect, it is unthinkable that the OPCW's final report lacks scientific durability. However, the fact that the OPCW did not directly refute the whistleblower's argument may have slightly worsened doubts about the OPCW. That Bellingcat refuted initially seemed strange, however, this also indicated that Bellingcat was functioning as part of a humanitarian network composed of the OPCW and human rights NGOs (at least in the case of Syria's chemical weapons issue). As such, the 2018 Douma incident raised serious issues about the authority of the OPCW, but the major Western media did not make enquiries deeply into this matter,[74] not judging the allegations against the OPCW to be serious. In that sense, this internal whistleblowing incident did not become a controversial issue, with little impact on the social credibility of the humanitarian network.

*

[72] Bellingcat, "The OPCW Douma Leaks Part 1: We Need To Talk About "Alex"", January 15, 2020, https://www.bellingcat.com/news/mena/2020/01/15/the-opcw-douma-leaks-part-1-we-need-to-talk-about-alex/.

[73] Bellingcat, "The OPCW Douma Leaks Part 2: We NeedTo Talk About Henderson," January 17, 2020, https://www.bellingcat.com/news/mena/2020/01/17/the-opcw-douma-leaks-part-2-we-need-to-talk-about-henderson/.

[74] Patrick Wintour, "Chemical Weapons Watchdog Defends Syria Report After Leaks," *The Guardian*, November 25, 2019; "Chemical Weapons Body Defends Syria Attack Conclusions After Leaks," *Reuters*, November 25, 2019.

The use of chemical weapons in war is a taboo in the international community, but they have been used in practice in wars after World War II. The Iran-Iraq War is a prime example, and this war greatly developed the humanitarian network for investigating chemical weapons. The conclusion of the Chemical Weapons Convention and the establishment of the OPCW were very important events in the generation of DAC. However, as the case of the Syrian conflict has shown, data on the use of chemical weapons is highly political, and even a network of experts including the OPCW could not avoid this political struggle.

Even when presenting scientifically robust data, there are countless rebuttals that can emerge. While disputes in academia can be peaceful, in the case of war, there is also the use of force such as air strikes, and depending on the content of the data, there is a possibility of creating more victims. Scientific disputes about war often made the internet a major battlefield, where Bellingcat played an active role. However, Bellingcat is not necessarily a hero of justice, nor is it infallible; it is a civic group that verifies scientific facts based on open sources, nothing more, nothing less. The truth about chemical weapons is always in the fog. To strain our eyes in this fog as much as possible, we have no choice but to carefully examine who and how the data on chemical weapons was investigated and published.

Conclusion: Is It Possible to Know the True Face of War?

This book has recorded and analyzed who created Data on Armed Conflicts (DAC) and how. Now, we turn our attention to examining the generation structure of the DAC. In the introduction, it was stated as a premise that data on international politics was often uncertain. For example, various researchers and practitioners argued that "in post-Cold War conflicts, eighty (or ninety) percent of the dead are civilians," but the data to substantiate this was unclear.

In response to the uncertainty of data, this book presents an approach called "critical functionalism," which relativizes the binary judgment of data as either true or false. It advocates thinking about how much scientific durability and social credibility data has, and what functions it serves. On top of that, it attempts to analyze how DAC is generated, its structure, and to draw a schematic of it.

Two Perception Filters

This book presents a model in which DAC is generated through two perception filters, and explains the structure of data generation accordingly. One is a filter called international norms. For example, the norm of protecting war casualties falls under this. The norm of protecting war casualties is the idea that in war, casualties should not be treated disrespectfully, and the protection of bodies and management of information is the duty of the warring nations. As analyzed in Chap. 2, this is based on the norm that even though one is a private soldier, the state has an obligation to explain what kind of death they suffered. The norm of protecting war casualties was developed from the nineteenth to the twentieth century and was codified. Furthermore, as seen in Chap. 3, after the codification of the norm of protecting war casualties, the norm of protecting civilians was codified in the 1949 Geneva Conventions, constituting civilians as "humans who must not be killed" under certain conditions. These norms determined the content of DAC. For example, the United Nations and NGOs that count the number of civilian deaths, and the mass media that report this information, select information based on these norms.

M. Igarashi, *War and Data on Armed Conflicts*, Evidence-Based Approaches to Peace and Conflict Studies 14, https://doi.org/10.1007/978-981-97-6418-1

The other perception filter is the scientific process. In this book, we covered areas such as statistical analysis, forensic analysis, and chemical analysis in Chaps. 5, 6, and 7 respectively. There, we revealed that experts form a global humanitarian network and generate scientific data on violations of international humanitarian law. As repeatedly emphasized throughout this book, scientific analysis necessitates the collaboration of diverse experts and specialized institutions, and it is not something that can be handled by the United Nations alone; therefore, to generate scientifically durable war data, a network connecting specialized institutions and experts around the world is necessary. The scientifically generated data, grounded in advanced expertise, was sometimes used as evidence in international criminal trials. However, because it is advanced, it often became difficult content that the general public could not understand.

Two Types of Actors

This book also focused on two types of actors in the analysis of the structure of war data generation. One is sovereign states, who were the main actors in generating DAC. The other is the humanitarian network, which this book intensively analyzed. The humanitarian network was formed by human rights NGOs, international organizations, scientific specialized institutions, etc., for purposes such as investigating violations of international humanitarian law and human rights law. Their DAC often aimed to specifically criticize sovereign states that violated international law, with the intention of applying pressure to stop acts of violation of humanitarian law.

As revealed in Chaps. 3 and 4, the Geneva Conventions, established in 1949, initially had almost no system in place to monitor their enforcement and, therefore, violations of humanitarian law by states were virtually unchecked. However, since the 1970s, NGOs that investigate and expose human rights abuses have gradually emerged, forming a global network and beginning to investigate and expose violations of international humanitarian law along with human rights law. The rapid development of such humanitarian networks was seen in the conflicts in Central and South America in the 1980s while in Chap. 4 we examined the birth of Human Rights Watch and the civil war in El Salvador as specific examples. In addition, the Physicians for Human Rights (PHR), which specializes in forensic medicine, was also formed through the struggle against Argentina's Dirty War.

The United Nations also began to gradually equip itself with institutional functions to investigate violations of humanitarian law along with human rights abuses since the 1960s. The UN Commission on Human Rights primarily undertook this function, with an early example the issue of occupied territories associated with the Third Arab-Israeli War. Furthermore, the United Nations enhanced its ability to investigate violations of humanitarian law through the establishment of the Office of the High Commissioner for Human Rights (OHCHR), the reorganization from the Commission on Human Rights to the Human Rights Council, and so on. From the perspective of enforcing international humanitarian law, the establishment of the International Criminal Court was an extremely important event, which opened the way to pursue legal responsibility for violations of humanitarian law in court. In addition, separate from this, the investigation mechanism regarding the use of chemical weapons has also developed since the 1980s.

Types of DAC

Through such theoretical frameworks, this book presents a variety of DAC, including the number of deaths in war (especially civilian deaths), the attributes and identities of victims, the causes of victims' deaths, and the weapons used (especially chemical weapons). In all these data, the most important thing was the testimonies and reports of the people involved. The dead cannot speak for themselves and, therefore, the first to convey information about the dead are the survivors who knew them. By gathering their testimonies and reports, it is possible to create a list of the dead and missing. With the completion of the list, the application of the Multiple Systems Estimation (MSE) and comparison with forensic investigation data became possible. Also, in the investigation of the use of chemical weapons, the testimonies of survivors who were at the scene became important evidence.

However, collecting testimonies and reports is not easy. It takes time and effort, and the local NGOs and other organizations that collect them often undertake such activities at great risk. The generation of DAC is fundamentally supported by such painstaking information collection activities. However, it can be difficult to disseminate information internationally solely through information gathering activities by local NGOs, while there may also be issues with scientific durability. There can be errors and duplications in testimonies and reports, and there may be victims that are not visible from these alone, which is where a global humanitarian network comes into play. Human rights NGOs, scientists, and even members of UN human rights-related organizations have been able to generate DAC that is scientifically durable and in accordance with human rights and humanitarian law by connecting with local networks. This data has in turn been disseminated worldwide through the media.

The opposite of this is fake news. For example, it has been pointed out that in Russia, there are "troll factories" that generate news to disrupt information on the internet. Elsewhere in the world, information that lacks scientific durability is being generated and disseminated[1] which has the exact opposite characteristics of the information disseminated through the humanitarian network. That is, while its scientific durability is significantly low, it is information that has the function of obstructing the establishment of facts or causing misrecognition of facts.

Three Indicators

Furthermore, this book presented three indicators to capture the characteristics of DAC: scientific durability, social trustworthiness, and the function of the data. The humanitarian network analyzed in this book has developed the ability to generate data with high scientific durability through various war investigations. Statistical methods

[1] Peter Pomerantsev, *This Is Not Propaganda: Adventures in the War against Reality* (London: Faber & Faber, 2019).

were applied to data on the number of war deaths, and rigorous forensic knowledge-based analysis was conducted in investigations into the identities and causes of death of the deceased. In investigations related to chemical weapons, analysis procedures in accordance with scientific rules were followed. However, not all DAC was free from criticism. In particular, there was intense debate among experts regarding chemical weapons. Nonetheless, even this debate served to enhance the scientific durability of the data.

Social trustworthiness was also a major issue. The number of deaths in war sometimes conflicted with local political and social interests, and in investigations into the identities and causes of death of the deceased, discrepancies with what the bereaved families sought caused friction. The use of chemical weapons sparked political controversy over who was responsible. No matter how scientifically durable it is, it cannot be the only persuasive material in the midst of political and social conflict. Scientific data is often specialized and difficult to understand, and is often difficult to be socially accepted.

In the end, the significance of DAC lies in its functionality: data for evidence in international trials, data to support political narratives, data to heal the hearts of bereaved families. Data has various purposes, and the content required for each is different. Therefore, it is not to be expected that there is such a thing as DAC that universally meets all needs. Researchers pursue objective data. It is natural for their profession, but it does not necessarily align with political and social needs.

Can We Know About War?

This book asked in the Introduction whether we can really know the true image of war from data. Based on the analysis so far, we might answer that we can only know about war partially from data. DAC is generated through at least two types of filters, which are useful for ensuring social meaning and scientific durability. However, it also means selectively cutting out the reality of war. Just because you know the number of war casualties does not mean you understand all of the tragedy of war, and just because you understand the trend of causes of death does not mean you have experienced the fear of war. What can be understood with scientifically durable data is only a small part of war. Analysis of data without full understanding may even distance us from the essence of war. It is like the allegory of Plato's cave.

However, even though we can only vaguely know about war through DAC, I do not think that DAC is meaningless. Hannah Arendt pointed out in her book *The Origins of Totalitarianism* that not only is human life taken away, but the ultimate form of violence is the erasure of the record that a person was alive.[2] Even though it is fragmentary, the fact that someone who was alive and then lost their life in war is recorded can be a way to save that person from the worst violence.

Things That Were Not Spoken

Unfortunately, this book was unable to analyze all DAC. Instead, it focused on DAC related to war casualties, including data on the number of deaths in war, the attributes

[2] Hannah Arendt, *The Origins of Totalitarianism* (London: Deutsch, 1986), Part 3.

and identities of the deceased, the causes of death, and the weapons used (such as chemical weapons). However, there are other important things in DAC, for example, data on violence against women, data on refugees, data on environmental impact, etc. These are also necessary data to know about war.

Furthermore, the war cases covered in this book are very limited. Examples related to the war that were not covered in this book include the case of Darfur in the 2000s (issues surrounding the number of deaths and genocide) and the cases of Afghanistan and Pakistan in the same decade (issues surrounding civilian collateral damage). Although considerable time was devoted to researching these issues in Afghanistan and Pakistan prior to the writing of this book, it was decided that they were not absolutely necessary for the book's purpose of drawing a schematic of DAC, and were therefore not included. After all, it is impossible to cover all wars, and choices must be made. I hope that readers will use the schematic presented in this book to analyze other war cases.

In addition, there are two points that this book did not sufficiently cover. The first is the impact of DAC by humanitarian networks on acts of violation of humanitarian law. Fact-finding often aims to criticize by name, but whether it leads to stopping, for example, the massacre of civilians is a significant issue. In the investigations of chemical weapons covered in this book (the Iran-Iraq War and the Syrian conflict), there was little evidence of deterrence, but what about in fact-finding as a whole? Also, this book analyzed the International Criminal Tribunal for the former Yugoslavia (ICTY) as an example of an international criminal court, but the cases of violations of international humanitarian law that come before international criminal courts are few, and it is questionable whether the possibility of trial actually leads to deterrence.

The second point is the impact of digitalization on DAC. Specifically, further investigation is needed on how much impact tweets by citizens and videos shot with smartphones have on the generation of DAC. For example, in the Syrian conflict, a vast amount of digital data is being collected and stored by citizen organizations and international organizations. Organizations such as the Commission for International Justice and Accountability (CIJA) and the Syrian Archive are involved in such activities, but what impact will they have on the issue of war crimes in the Syrian conflict in the future? There are also cases where children's tweets during wartime have a significant political and social impact on social networks, and analysis of such phenomena is also necessary.[3]

Nevertheless, I hope that this book has been able to present some meaningful schematic of DAC. At least after reading this book, the DAC that appears in the media should look different than before. Who generated that data, how, and for what purpose? What historical process led to its generation? The one to think about it is you.

---

[3] David Patrikarakos, *War in 140 Characters: How Social Media Is Reshaping Conflict in the Twenty-First Century* (New York: Basic Books, 2017); Omar Al-Ghazzi, "An Archetypal Digital Witness: The Child Figure and the Media Conflict over Syria," *International Journal of Communication* 13 (2019); Kari Andén-Papadopoulos, "Citizen Camera-Witnessing: Embodied Political Dissent in the Age of "Mediated Mass Self-Communication"", *New Media & Society* 16, no. 5 (2014).

Index

M. Igarashi, *War and Data on Armed Conflicts*, Evidence-Based Approaches to Peace and Conflict Studies 14, https://doi.org/10.1007/978-981-97-6418-1

The manufacturer's authorised representative in the EU is Springer Nature Customer Service Centre GmbH, Europaplatz 3, 69115 Heidelberg, Germany. If you have any concerns regarding our products, please contact ProductSafety@springernature.com

Printed and bound by CPI Group (UK) Ltd, Croydon, CR0 4YY
01/10/2026
02225876-0011